Ankush Days

the story of Ishtiaq
mahout of Corbett Tiger Reserve

AQEEL FAROOQI

Oh, my Lord! Expand for me my chest and make my task easy. Remove the impediment from my speech, so that they may understand what I say…

~ the Prayer of Moses

This book is dedicated to all those
who love Corbett National Park,
and especially to those who have had
the pleasure of experiencing
an elephant safari with Ishtiaq.

Copyright

ANKUSH DAYS
© 2022, Aqeel Farooqi
Email: farooqi.aqeel@gmail.com
Lucknow (Uttar Pradesh),

All rights reserved

Cover Credit
Roopendra, Graphic Artist

The Ankush

 The **'ankush'** is the primary tool employed by mahouts to control elephants. It consists of a sharp hook attached to a 3 feet iron rod, ending in a pointed spear. It is also called 'elephant goad' or 'bull-hook'.

The ankush first appeared in India in the 5th century BC and has been used ever since by mahouts to train and drive elephants.

Since this book is about the life of a mahout, it is titled **'Ankush Days'**

Disclaimer

This book is based on extensive conversations I had with Ishtiaq during the times I spent with him. These were further augmented by his narratives which I recorded in his native language and dialect. I have used these to try and weave his life's story around them.

The events and persons that he mentioned in his narratives were recollections drawn from his memory. They may digress a little here and there from the versions stated by others, but different versions will always remain open to debates on perspectives and points of view

On my part, I have tried to seek corroboration of the events from either the persons concerned or from acceptable documented records.

Care has been taken to keep the story true to Ishtiaq's narratives. It is definitely not meant to be a critique or to cause offense to any person, living or dead.

In mentioning the names of the persons who figure in this book, I have done away with their titles and salutations for the sake of brevity and seamless flow of syntax. But my respect and regards for those seniors are beyond doubt, and I place it on record here.

Aqeel Farooqi

Acknowledgements

I have to thank many people who helped me in the writing of this book.

The first is my friend Dr SM Tariq. He loved Ishtiaq as much as I did, and I consider him as my long-time collaborator in this project. We conceived it together, and prepared the grounds for its execution together. During my long years of dithering in the writing of this book, he was always there, goading me on. It took time Tariq, but here it is now, for whatever it is worth.

I thank my wife Noreen for her infinite patience with me in letting me do all that I want to, and then quietly taking care of all the responsibilities that should have been mine. Sorry for all that my dear, but that's the way the cookie had to crumble for you.

I am thankful to Dr Asad R. Rahmani, eminent wildlife scientist, and former Director BNHS, for being kind enough to read the manuscript and write a foreword. He has always been my guiding light and I have looked up to him as a mentor during the long time I have known him.

I must thank Mr Mohammed Ahsan IFS, who at one time served as Director Corbett Park, and shared with me his viewpoints on the inherent characteristics of a mahout's life. His encouragement to me was invaluable, and he let me freely draw excerpts from his books with references to the tigers Sheroo and Dhitoo.

My thanks go out to Mr AN Singh, the long-serving Research Officer of Corbett Park, for his fond wishes and encouragement in the writing of the book. Since he figured so prominently in many of the incidents mentioned here, I sought his corroboration on many of Ishtiaq's narratives.

My special thanks are reserved for Mr Sanjay Kumar, IAS currently posted as Secretary Finance, Govt of U.P. His sharp acumen as a bureaucrat is equally matched by his love for forests and wildlife. His moral support was unstinted during the writing of this book.

I am also thankful to my friends Rustam, Lippoo and Sadiq from Katni (MP), Saad bin Asif from Sherkot, and Faisal Husain from Lucknow, who are my constant companions and drive me around in their jaunty jalopies whenever I want to be lost in our favourite forests of UP and MP.

I wish to record my thanks to Sapphire Infraventures Pvt. Ltd. Lucknow for their benevolent support in the publishing of this book, to Roopendra, Graphic Artist for the cover design and to Ishtiaq's son Irfan Ahmed, for giving me access to some of the photographs used in the book.

I am indebted to Santhosh Paul, a copy-editor from Kochi who acquired a copy of the book and used his keen eye to suggest edits as he read on. You are now an integral part of the book Santhosh, and I thank you for your unstinted help.

Aqeel Farooqi

Foreword 1
by
Dr Asad R. Rahmani
Wildlife Scientist & Former Director, BNHS

In the Indian forests, elephants have always played a great role, first for towing timber, taking '*sahibs*' for shikar, general patrolling, and transport on unmotorable areas, but now mainly for taking tourists for wildlife viewing, particularly tiger or rhino. Mahouts, without whom elephants cannot work, come at the lowest rung of the hierarchy, despite their significant role in the forest department.

There is a preternatural relationship between a mahout and his elephant. Most mahouts treat an elephant as an overgrown child, a part of the family, a psychological anchor without which life is incomplete. Fortunately, the intelligent animal also reciprocates, perhaps to a much greater degree. There are incidences where an elephant has stopped eating when his mahout falls sick or dies.

Most forest officers whom I know, treat mahouts and their elephants with great respect. In many national parks, there is a tradition that when the Field Director comes to camp, he/she feeds the elephants. There are vets in the forest department who specialize in the treatment of elephants, and they are in great demand since treating elephants is a specialized subject.

I love elephants and think that they are one of the most beautiful animals when seen in the wild. The elephant's grace and elegance is however lost in the urban environment when they are seen on crowded Indian streets being made to beg for alms by their hard-hearted owners. The forest department elephants are in much better condition than the temple elephants, and they get a lot of freedom. Some are even 'retired' after serving the forest department for 40-45 years and a pension is sanctioned for their upkeep. Pregnant females are given maternity leave from routine duties and given a special diet by caring forest officers and mahouts. A newborn calf is not only a bundle of joy for the elephant fraternity, but for the entire forest staff.

Aqeel Farooqi has done a great service by writing a book on the legendary mahout Ishtiaq Ahmad of the UP Forest Department. Ishtiaq was an indomitable and unique character, admired and liked by anyone who came in contact with him. His knowledge about Corbett Park, its wild animals, and their behaviour was astounding. He was a mahout much-sought by many 'VIPs' coming to Corbett Park, and some would even book him in advance.

It is clear from the book that the writer was in awe of Ishtiaq. After reading the book, it is also clear that Aqeel has an eye for details, and an unpretentious narrative style. While reading the book, it reminded me of Mushi Prem Chand's stories - simple, no flowery language, short sentences, no jargon - but great description. Anyone can relate to Prem Chand's stories. Similarly, I could relate to the places and people mentioned in this book, as I knew many forest officers or have visited the places where Ishtiaq spent most of his life.

This book again proves that a good writer can weave a story on a very simple subject like the life of a mahout, with all his trials and tribulations, into an eminently readable book. I am sure, like Ishtiaq Ahmad, there are equally good mahouts in other parts of India. Will anyone take up their stories as Aqeel has so wonderfully done?

Lucknow   **(Asad R. Rahmani)**

Foreword 2

by
Mohammed Ahsan, IFS
Former Principal Chief Conservator of Forests, UP

Ankush Days is the story of a legendary mahout named Ishtiaq, who served in different parts of the terai forests. However, his longest innings was at Dhikala, the main camp of Corbett National Park. In my two short tenures in Corbett Park, first in 1980-82 and then as Director in 1999-2000, I had the good fortune of knowing Ishtiaq, but my busy schedule at my headquarters Ramnagar, and other official engagements, precluded me from knowing Ishtiaq as intimately as the writer of this book and my friend Aqeel Farooqi has known him.

An expert tracker of wild animals, Ishtiaq was part of many operations of liquidation of man-eating tigers and other dangerous animals for about half a century that he served in the forest department. He was always in demand by forest officials, licensed shikaris, VIPs, their guests, and common visitors. His knowledge and handling of jungle terrain, particularly of Corbett Park, was marvelous, the ease with which he handled his elephants was remarkable, and his lore about the habits and habitats of wild animals was second to none.

Aqeel has beautifully depicted how the bonds between men and animals develop when they work together for a common cause. Ankush Days is a beautiful story of a bond between Ishtiaq and his longest-serving elephant Rambha. She is like a child to Ishtiaq. When Rambha is passing through unbound throes of death, Ishtiaq cries as a father would do at the agony of his child.

Ishtiaq, as per Aqeel's version, was a veritable storehouse of knowledge about forests and wild animals. My opinion is that the way he made Ishtiaq speak about his life and times, and various incidences of shikar and liquidation of man-eating tigers, Aqeel has turned his book into something like a precious document relating to those times, and whenever someone would sit down to write the history of conservation of wildlife in the terai areas of Uttar Pradesh and Uttaranchal, he would have no option but to consult Aqeel's book.

Ankush Days is an invaluable document and a missing link to so many obscure - yet very important, undocumented or insufficiently documented events and happenings in and around Corbett Park. The details of these events are good interpretations of wildlife biology and human psychology. Aqeel has done lots of recreating of history through Ishtiaq. The way Aqeel prods Ishtiaq and makes him speak can only be the job of a professional.

Aqeel's book is also not just a plain narration of what Ishtiaq tells of his life, his job, his officers, his shikar anecdotes, the extermination of many man-eating tigers, but it has many humane aspects too.

If there was a powerful, indelible bond between Ishtiaq and his elephant Rambha, I find another bond between Aqeel and Ishtiaq, a bond of friendship, affection, empathy, mutual concern, and human relationship. The first chapter of the book wherein Aqeel and his friend Dr Tariq, the orthopedic surgeon, are waiting for Ishtiaq at Charbagh railway station, and finally, a frail man apparently in great pain, walks towards them slowly and steadily, is poignant enough to move even a hard-hearted person.

Ishtiaq belonged to a family where the mahout's occupation or *mahoutgiri* was a family tradition. Handling and driving elephants were in his blood. So was the call of the jungle. When he had a bad time during his career and had to leave the forest department for few years, it was the call of the jungle that drove him back to the forests and take up *mahoutgiri* once more. He was a man of courage, confidence, valor and goodwill, who never treated anyone ever with contempt.

However, Ishtiaq's life was not all thrill, adventure, or pleasure of living a glorious jungle life. It was much more, often sweet, but often sour. His life is also the tale of living on the edge of penury, hardship, debt, and personal tragedies. His most favorite elephant Rambha died a painful death. He could never come out of the nightmare of this loss. His favorite officers and bosses retired one after the other. His young son met the fatal tragedy of being bitten by a king cobra on a dark night at Dhikala. Ishtiaq, handicapped by limited communication and transport, even with his best efforts, could not take him to appropriate medical aid, and the son breathed his last in Ishtiaq's embrace.

This tragedy jolted his daughter, younger by a year to this deceased boy, so much that the girl died within two months of her brother's death. And this double tragedy completely broke Ishtiaq down. At the fag end of his career, he was a frail-looking old man, struggling for survival. That is how time often treats men of valor, courage, and adventure.

Ankush Days has covered many aspects. Aqeel has done a laudable job of telling the story of a member of the mahout clan, a section of the society that is most neglected socially and economically. The forest department is gradually giving up its tradition of stationing elephants for its inspection works except in the national parks and sanctuaries - there too for monitoring or rescue work.

Most of its mahouts have become old and disheartened. In the coming days, there might not be many energetic and competent mahouts around. Their living condition is bad. They are overworked and underpaid. Their duties are perilous as well as strenuous. Their skills are not fully appreciated in modern times. No wonder then that their progeny might not like to join the family tradition of *mahoutgiri*.

Fact is, most of the mahouts working in forest conditions have so many tales under their sleeves to tell but there are not many listeners. Everyone is in a hurry. Ishtiaq was lucky in the sense that not only he was extraordinary in his professional conduct but fortunate in having a listener like Aqeel Farooqi. Not that the other mahouts are less competent than Ishtiaq - I have no wish to disparage any one of them - but probably they were prisoners of their own circumstances and could not find their own 'Aqeel Farooqi'.

Aqeel's book is a pioneer in touching the life of mahouts. To the best of my knowledge, no writer has ever done what Aqeel could do – making a hero out of a mahout. The book may also be treated as a tribute to the delicate, dangerous, and esoteric occupation of mahouts.

At the cost of repetition let me again emphasize that the book is a storehouse of knowledge and a missing link in the history of wildlife conservation in the region of *terai*. Ankush Days is not just the plain narration of a mahout about many incidents but is sufficiently dotted with wit and humour.

And in the end, Aqeel's bonding and jelling with Ishtiaq is laudable and highlights the humane side of his character. It's every third day that Aqeel rushes off to some jungle to shake off the dust of urban life strewn over him. Such a man can't be anything but sensitive. And his book Ankush Days amply reflects that.

Lucknow   **(Mohammed Ahsan, IFS)**

Foreword 3

by
Ajit Narain Singh
Former Research Officer, Corbett Tiger Reserve

I was pleasantly surprised to know that Ankush Days has been written on Ishtiaq Ahmed, the legendary mahout who served for a long time in Corbett national park. The book has traced Ishtiaq's personal life, and also touched upon many important events that occurred in Corbett national park during the period when Ishtiaq was serving there. There is no doubt that Ishtiaq was an amazing storyteller, and his stories have found a great platform in this book

I have had the privilege of being posted as a Research Officer in Corbett Park for almost ten years. During my posting, I was also involved in resolving many man-animal conflict situations that the park management was faced with. Whenever trapping or tranquilization was not an option, I had to resort to elimination of man-eating tigers on the orders of the government. It was during such assignments that Ishtiaq's mastery of jungle lore and his vast experience in the handling of elephants, used to be of immense help in the execution of such assignments.

I learned a lot about jungle lore from Ishtiaq in addition to the intricate art of tracking wild animals, and the ecology and behavior of tigers. I congratulate the author Aqeel Farooqi for choosing to write a book on Ishtiaq, and sincerely hope it will serve the purpose of keeping alive the memories of this truly remarkable man.

Lucknow   **(Ajit Narain Singh)**

Contents

CHAPTER 1

Prologue

It is a hot and humid July morning as I stand on platform number 4 of Lucknow railway station. With me is my friend Dr SM Tariq, an orthopaedic surgeon practicing in Lucknow. Both of us have been up early today in order to reach the railway station, and are now anxiously awaiting the arrival of the train that will bring an important guest from Dhikala, which is the main tourist encampment located in the deep recesses of the famous Corbett Tiger Reserve.

As we wait for the train, the oppressively hot and humid weather squeezes out cascades of sweat that runs down our faces, while the smells and sounds emanating from the multitude on the platform assail our senses. However, these small discomforts seem to pale into insignificance in the face of the heightened expectation of meeting our guest.

The train rattles into the station, and the waiting passengers go into a frenzy, their sudden flurry of activity creating a sort of dismembered Mexican wave, as they surge forward to board the train. We are aware that it would be difficult to pinpoint our guest in this melee, and so prefer to stand near the exit, hoping to meet him there.

Fortunately, it does not take us long to spot him. He is a wizened man, walking slowly towards us. His left hand holds a cheap walking cane for support, while the right hand is shrivelled and twisted, fingers held stiffly against his chest. But he is making use of that limb too, his single piece of baggage - a plastic shopping bag - hanging on it. As he walks towards us, we cannot help but notice how frail and puny he looks in these urban surroundings - a far cry from the strong healthy man we knew, a man who has spent most of his life literally riding a colossus.

As we hug him affectionately, he responds with his characteristic ear-to-ear grin, amply conveying his happiness at meeting us. Although we are also overwhelmed with pleasure, we are more than a wee bit worried about the respective responsibilities that my friend and I have taken upon ourselves when we invited this man to come to Lucknow.

The little prickle of doubt that nags us is how effectively would we be able to fulfil those responsibilities. On his part, Tariq has to get to work and use all his orthopaedic and physiotherapeutic skills to get his limbs working again, while I have to glean out every detail of his life, to be able to weave his life's story in such a way that it honestly brings out a clear image of this truly remarkable man.

He is a veritable storehouse of jungle lore, and an excellent raconteur of jungle tales drawn from his lifetime experience of forest life. His humour, wit and dialect are unmatched, and when he holds forth on exciting stories of the 'tayger' - as he pronounces tiger - it is spell-binding

The man is Ishtiaq Ahmed, a mahout *par excellence*. And this is his story.

CHAPTER 2

How it all began

The idea of writing the story of Ishtiaq's life was not a premeditated one but was conceived on the basis of a spur-of-the-moment decision. In April 2002, Tariq and I were returning from Corbett Park after having spent three eventful wildlifing days there. Before starting from Dhikala, we had paid a visit to Ishtiaq's shack to enquire about his health and to have a quiet tête-à-tête with him. We knew that Ishtiaq had recently suffered elongated bouts of illness, which had left him partially crippled in both his hands and feet.

He was glad to see us. Based on our long acquaintance with him, he knew that we were his friends and admirers who cared about him. In our presence, he did not have to be either ashamed or rueful about the condition he was in. While Tariq commenced his examination, pushing and pulling diagnostically at all his joints, Ishtiaq cheerfully kept up an often-interrupted conversation with us.

It was clear from his animated speech and glinting eyes that his present debility had neither dampened his spirits nor diminished his inherent enthusiasm for recounting wildlife stories. It was characteristic of this large-hearted man that he had refused to let this huge physical setback pin him down. He responded to the examination with fortitude and stoical patience, although it was quite evident from his occasional winces that he was in great distress and pain.

Of this incident, Tariq recalls, *"at that time Ishtiaq was down with tuberculosis of his neck vertebrae which had caused paralysis of all his four limbs. He was still in service in those days, hence residing in his home in Dhikala. On getting this news, we had gone to Dhikala to check him out. There he was, spread-eagled on his bed with his wife beside him. He was paralyzed from his neck downwards but there wasn't a hint of defeat in his demeanour. He told us he was under treatment from AIIMS Delhi, and that he felt a marginal recovery.*

Even in this condition, Ishtiaq being Ishtiaq, he had an anecdote for us, and it was about his elephant Rambha. He told us that once in a blue moon Rambha used to become temperamental and stubborn, and refused to listen to him. It was then that his wife used to come to the fore, and dealt effectively with Rambha to bring her around. Ishtiaq's wife was a quaint Rampuri lady, dressed in a gharara and a no-nonsense attitude. She would not let us leave her house without a cup of chai, which she prepared for us. Meanwhile, Ishtiaq managed to raise a few laughs even in this condition. Much later he recovered enough to become mobile again, albeit with a walking stick".

At the end of his examination, Tariq was of the view that lack of proper medicines and physiotherapy had taken their toll, and much of the advantage associated with pinpoint diagnosis and early treatment had been lost. In his opinion, the chances of Ishtiaq attaining full and unhindered movement of his right hand were not very high, although the stiffness of his other limbs could be rectified to some extent.

Nevertheless, we did want to give ourselves the chance of having him treated, all the while hoping fervently that Ishtiaq's strong willpower and resilience would go a long way in enhancing and supplementing the response to the treatment given to him even at this late stage. We had therefore extended an invitation to Ishtiaq, asking him to come to Lucknow as soon as he could, so that we could have him examined and placed under treatment in a bid to arrest the loss of sensation and use of his extremities. He had obliged us by cheerfully promising that he would come soon after the Corbett Park tourist season ended in June.

During our journey back to Lucknow, we discussed our approach to Ishtiaq's treatment when he did come to Lucknow. Our discussions reassured us that it would not be a problem to have him examined by the best consultants and put on physiotherapy and medication. That apprehension taken care of, we laughingly admitted that as a bonus, we would be getting to hear a lot of interesting jungle tales from Ishtiaq while he was with us.

It was then that the idea of writing Ishtiaq's story struck me. If we were going to have Ishtiaq with us for some time, why not get him to talk about his experiences, and then maybe I could try and document his life and times for the benefit of many others like me, who held Ishtiaq in high esteem and might want to read about the events of his life.

When he arrived at Lucknow three months later, it was a whirlwind of activity that followed. As soon as I mentioned my intention of documenting his life, he agreed. It seemed to me that somewhere in his heart, he had always wanted a book written about him.

But it had to be first things first. The primary requirement of his medical examination and pathological tests were taken care of, and medication started. He was then given regular physiotherapy sessions, which were interspersed with elongated sessions of video recordings which served the dual purpose of enthralling us with the anecdotes and incidents in his life, as well as providing us a video recording that would serve as a repository which I could draw from when I got down to writing about him.

As we recorded his story in his dialect and words, we found that some incidents were funny, while others were cloaked in sadness. He spoke of his early days and family, of tiger *shikar* when it was allowed, of man-eating tigers he helped to be shot or captured, and of the trials and tribulations of his family during the long years he spent in the Corbett Park as a mahout. He strongly berated and castigated a few people at times, but also spoke with respect and admiration for a lot of other persons.

At the time of writing, I realized that most of the people he mentioned have now passed away, so I took care not to mention anything that reflects adversely on any person, living or dead. In his conversations with me, he was candid enough to give expression to his most personal thoughts, and it sometimes felt strange being privy to his viewpoint about people and events which tended to vary so drastically from that which is universally known and believed.

However, it came across as a matter of wonderment to me that a man who was singularly instrumental in providing great moments of thrill and excitement to countless others when he took them out into the forests for their rendezvous with the elusive Indian tiger, had himself lived such a simple and spartan life.

This book then, is my tribute to a man who I have looked upon as a friend since the last thirty-five years of my life. To me, he was never just a low-paid government employee whose job it was to take pompous tourists out on an elephant safari into the forests. On the contrary, he was a sensitive human being, a wise old man who was a veritable storehouse of jungle lore that may not be found documented in any book.

I do not doubt that like me, there are many other Corbett park-goers who knew Ishtiaq and feel the same about him, and they too would want his memory and legacy to survive for posterity.

It is from them that I hope to receive validation that my effort to make Ishtiaq live for eternity has not been in vain.

CHAPTER 3

Ishtiaq & Rambha - A team par excellence

It was a cold February morning in 1985 when I started on a jungle safari with Ishtiaq, astride his elephant named Rambha. The sun had still not breached the horizon, but a surreal light from the east was bathing the forests of Dhikala with a suffused reddish glow.

Our route took us through the misty grassland around the Dhikala camp, and on to the watchtower on the Sambhar Road. From there we made the slow descent down to the Ramganga river, crossing it leisurely as Rambha stopped every few steps to take in a trunkful of water and push it into her mouth. She seemed to be in no hurry to leave the water, and Ishtiaq quite happily allowed her to have her fill. Once the river was eventually crossed, we entered the great expanse of grassland and scrub forest lying beyond.

Ishtiaq was now peering intently at the ground below, to pick up any visual sign of the tiger's movement. He had been informed by other mahouts that a tiger had been sighted in the vicinity last evening, and there were chances that it could be encountered again this morning. It was not long before we were provided with ample evidence of the tiger's proximity.

Suddenly chital and grassland birds started giving alarm calls, and a strange transformation came over Ishtiaq and the rest of us. We were now alert to the definite presence of the tiger, and our eyes and ears were in a highly receptive state. We could see Ishtiaq tugging and pulling with his knees at Rambha's neck, and she quickly responded to his motions.

It was not long before Ishtiaq's piercing gaze picked out the lithe form of the tiger lying full length in the thick grass, trying his best to avoid being seen by the intruders. Remember, those were times when tigers behaved like tigers, with elusiveness and secrecy, and it was quite a rarity for us to see a wild tiger, unlike the present time when in most national parks, tigers virtually parade before lines of vehicles laden with noisy, chattering tourists.

Having now been located and sighted by us, the tiger's first instinct was to make a hasty retreat from the spot, which he did with feline speed. We saw him slithering off, and was immediately lost to sight. We were quite disappointed at this brief encounter, but Ishtiaq was not one to be fended off so quickly. He indicated to us that he was still on the tiger's trail, and urgently made Rambha follow the direction the tiger had taken.

But the tiger had moved deep into the elephant grass, and it now seemed difficult to dislodge him from there. Although we could still see him indistinctly, a deep nullah prevented us from going any nearer for that vital photograph that I still hadn't been able to get. It was here that the intricate combination of mahout and elephant revealed itself. Ishtiaq motioned to me to stay ready with my camera, while his toes sent silent directives to Rambha.

In response, the snaking trunk lifted a huge clod of wet mud and sent it flying across the dividing nullah, landing in a spray on the recalcitrant tiger. Alarmed, or probably angry at this ignominy, out he came roaring in a mock charge, canines fully bared. For those few moments, the humans clearly perceived the terror that must strike a tiger's prey when that striped mass of muscle and fury launches into that final assault.

It may have lasted seconds, but was enough to freeze our blood. Thankfully, the fingers worked away in reflex to give our cameras the everlasting impressions of a charging tiger.

"Wah wah Ishtiaq, wah Rambha wah, shabaash!" went the rounds of congratulations and thanksgiving, showered excitedly on the mahout and his charge, following this magnificent sighting of the elusive tiger.

The charging tiger

Ishtiaq and Rambha. A mahout-elephant combination *par excellence*. For all serious visitors to the famous Corbett National Park, an elephant safari with Ishtiaq is a unique experience. An excellent tracker, he deftly reads the signs left by the denizens of the forest from atop his lofty perch on Rambha's neck. And when during the ride, the situation does not warrant absolute silence, in his own inimitable style and dialect, Ishtiaq will give you a lesson or two in jungle lore that you are not likely to find in any book.

Being the most sought-after pair for an elephant safari in Corbett Park, he and his elephant have perforce taken many a pompous VIP into the forest, but for the average wildlife enthusiast like me, Ishtiaq was the *maitre d'safari*, the master of the situation, easily striking a balance of camaraderie and strictness with the tourists, while out on his two excursions each day.

I have had the privilege of being a close friend of Ishtiaq ever since my visits to Corbett started in 1985. Initially going out with any mahout that happened to be allotted to me, I gradually learnt to distinguish between the good ones and the average ones. This process of elimination finally resulted in short-listing a couple of mahouts like Nazir and Nawab. And of course, Ishtiaq.

My personal choice, however, tilted easily towards Ishtiaq, and a large part of that preference was determined by his elephant, Rambha. She was sure-footed and steady on all kinds of terrain. Right from the time one started from camp astride her, one felt brave and confident of facing the tiger on its own ground. Never known to have backed off or panicked, she easily conveyed her confidence to the riders through her studied nonchalance during tiger sightings. Even if there were no sightings of the big cat, the ride itself was always eventful. And so, year after year, I returned to Corbett for the inevitable rendezvous with my human and pachyderm friend.

Those were days when Corbett Park was a part of undivided Uttar Pradesh, with the Forest Department headquarters located at Lucknow. Since I was also a state government officer posted at Lucknow, it was quite easy for me to secure entry permits and room bookings at Corbett Park whenever I wanted.

As the frequency of my annual visits to Corbett Park grew, so also did my friendship with most of the staff posted there. This instilled in me a sense of belonging to the place and made my visits much more fruitful because of the extended periods of time I used to spend there.

Then came an interlude when my preoccupations with more frequent visits to Bandhavgarh and Kanha national parks, didn't leave me time to go to Corbett Park for almost two years. Castigating myself for this lapse in loyalty to my most favourite forest, I finally squeezed in a trip to Corbett during end-January 1998.

The thrill of reaching Dhikala after such a long time was as exhilarating as ever. It was freezing cold at Dhikala that year, but the welcoming hugs from the modest staff members were so warm that they dispelled the biting cold of the season. But tragic news was at hand. "Rambha is dying," they told me. It was shocking and unbelievable. Elephants have long lives, we've been told. How could she die, she was only seventy?

We made a beeline for the place where Rambha was lying sick and helpless. The very first sight of the fallen giant made me falter. She was lying on her left side. The ground where she lay had been scraped and muddied by her vain efforts to stand upright. A bonfire was burning nearby to ward off the cold from her, as well as the humans attending on her. There was Ishtiaq, his wife and children, the Range Officer Kundan Singh Rawat, and a motley group of other mahouts and *characuts*. All had genuine concern on their faces. An elephant for a mahout is not an animal, but a family member. And here, a family member was dying.

Ishtiaq stood up and met me without speaking. The grim situation before us did not warrant any speech, even though we were meeting after a long time. We silently walked up to where Rambha's head lay and squatted on our haunches close to her. The only eye visible on that gaunt face followed us. While I stroked her feeble trunk with sadness, Ishtiaq reached out and wiped the trickling discharge from under her eye. "*Na beta, mat ro. Bahut dard ho raha hai kya* ?" he asked (No child, don't cry. Are you in great pain?). I also felt the start of a warm trickle on my face that needed wiping, and I did that furtively.

Later, sitting on a *charpoy* near the blazing fire where Rambha lay, I finally managed to piece together the events that were about to deprive Corbett National Park of one of its most well-known treasures.

Soon after Corbett Park closed for the monsoons in June last year, a wild tusker started making frequent forays into the Dhikala encampment. Probably emboldened by the lack of tourist activity, or maybe spurred on by the enticing smell of the female riding elephants in the camp, he repeatedly targeted the *feelkhana* or stables where the elephants were housed.

More often than not, he was driven off before he could actually enter, but on 16th July, he did manage to sneak in, and in the ensuing melee, drove a tusk into Rambha's right ear. The wound was not severe, but it took time to heal. During treatment, she was quartered at Dhangarhi Gate and Bijrani, from where she returned to Dhikala in November, in time for the start of another busy tourist season. But not being certified fully fit by the vet, she remained off duty.

It was on the fateful night of 4th November that the wild tusker raided the *feelkhana* again. Possibly due to panic because of her last encounter with him, she jerked frantically at the hobble chain restraining her hind leg, breaking it by sheer effort.

The commotion culminated with Range Officer Rawat firing in the air and scaring off the tusker. But in the effort of breaking the chain, something in Rambha's leg snapped too. According to Ishtiaq, it was not a broken bone, nor even a dislocation. It was some vital nerve that suffered a traumatic injury, resulting in the leg getting inflamed and bloated out of all proportion.

Getting to work with his indigenous and native remedies, Ishtiaq treated and nursed her leg for almost one month. Rambha showed signs of recovery, the inflammation on her leg subsided, but she didn't attain full fitness.

Doctors from Pantnagar gave her a check-up on 21st January, and prescribed tonics and calcium tablets in a bid to speed up her recovery. But that probably was not ordained. She stopped eating her rations from the next day, despite all efforts from her human friends to coerce or force-feed her.

Six days of starvation for an ailing elephant took their toll, and on the morning of 27th January, she fell forward heavily on her face. That, according to Ishtiaq, was an ominous sign. All her desperate efforts to get up, even with the support of the puny human hands, sapped whatever little energy that may have been left in her emaciated frame.

Nayyar, a forest department staffer, gave her two bottles of intravenous glucose, but it was already too late. By the time I arrived at Dhikala at noon that day, all hopes had been lost, and when I sat down near her with Ishtiaq, we were just two of a group of helpless onlookers desolately awaiting the passing of a gentle forest giant.

While we sat near her late into the night, Rambha's death throes continued. She kept writhing and stretching her legs again and again. Each movement resulted in a discharge of urine, indicating that her sphincter muscles had succumbed to the weakness. But not once did she utter a sound.

When Ishtiaq's son Irfan, tried to push in a lump of *gur* (jaggery) into her mouth, she weakly twirled her trunk around his arm and clearly told him not to do so. And so, all that her human retinue could do was to stoke the bonfire to keep it burning warmly, and to keep adjusting the huge cotton *gadda* (mattress) that was her protection from the night dew, and which repeatedly kept falling off her jerky, twitching body.

Before retiring to my room for the night, I stroked her gently for the last time, and promised myself that I would not go near her again, and thus avoid seeing her in mortal agony. The thrill of coming to Corbett after such a long gap had transformed into sadness, and even the sighting of a magnificent male tiger that crossed from under the Sambhar Road *machan*, failed to dissipate the gloom.

The next morning, I was told that she had spent the night in great discomfort and that the road-gang labourers had been requisitioned to start digging the pit that would be her grave. Not feeling brave enough to face the end, I drove away from Dhikala the same morning, foolishly comforting myself that I had left her alive, and hoping that by some miracle, she just might survive after all.

But the miracle never happened, and the dreaded news finally arrived when Suresh Pant, a Dhikala staff member, came to Lucknow to visit me.

Rambha died at 8.45 PM on the 28th of January 1998. Her gaunt body was laid to rest at the very spot where she had fallen down to breathe her last. Ishtiaq's companion of fourteen years, and the favourite elephant of countless wildlife enthusiasts coming to Corbett Park, had finally passed on to the Happy Hunting Grounds.

CHAPTER 4

Ishtiaq's Family

It will be worthwhile to touch upon the details of Ishtiaq's family, both on his paternal as well as maternal side. It emerges that many of his family elders were mahouts involved with the profession of elephant driving. None of them was highly placed in the economic sense of the word, but I am sure that the mention of their names and vocation will give the reader an idea of how Ishtiaq's family tree was branched.

PATERNAL SIDE

	Ali Hasan	Ishtiaq's paternal grandfather. He had two sons.
1	**Dulha Hasan**	**Ishtiaq's father.** He was earlier a mahout in the elephant stables of the Nawab of Rampur. Was subsequently employed in the Forest Department.
2	Maseeta	Ishtiaq's uncle. He was a *saathmaar* (a sort of elephant picador) in the elephant stables of Nawab of Rampur.

MATERNAL SIDE

	Hidayat Ali	Ishtiaq's maternal grandfather. He was a mahout in the elephant stables of Nawab of Rampur. Later he became a mahout in the Forest Department. He had four sons and three daughters.
1	Himayat Ali	He was a bearer with Chief Conservator WA Bailey (1940-41). After Bailey's death, he became a coal contractor. Then worked as a mahout in the Silviculture and Working Plan Division of the Forest Department.

2	Latafat Ali	He was a mahout and an expert in *shikar* arrangements. He worked with CB Singh, IFS when he was DFO Ramnagar, and later the Director of Corbett Park. Ishtiaq was under his tutelage as a teenager and learnt much about elephant care and management from Latafat Ali.
3	Liaqat Ali	He had a shoe shop in Ramnagar
4	Izafat Ali	He was visually impaired since birth. He was a *Hafiz-e-Quran* (memorizer of the Quran) and earned his living by teaching it to children.
5	**Maseeti Begum**	**Ishtiaq's mother.** She was married to Dulha Hasan, Ishtiaq's father
6	Khushnudi Begum	Married to **Azmat Ali,** a mahout posted in the Governor's retinue. Their daughter **Razia Begum** was married to Ishtiaq.
7	Kaneez Begum	She was married to a government employee in Rampur.

Ishtiaq's parents **Dulha Hasan** and **Maseeti Begum** had five sons and three daughters.

1	Nabi Jan	The eldest son was a vagabond and never worked in a regular job.
2	Ali Jan	He died at the age of 7 years from an affliction of smallpox.
3	Niaz Ahmed	He was a born paraplegic and therefore remained unemployed
4	**Ishtiaq Ahmed**	He served in the Forest Department as a mahout for most of his life.

5	Akhlaq Ahmed	He was a *characut* in the Ramnagar and Haldwani Forest Division. Left the job and went on to become a mason.
6	Laeequn	Ishtiaq's sister, now deceased.
7	Shafeequn	Ishtiaq's sister, now deceased.
8	Shakeela	This sister is the only one still alive. She lives in Bareilly. She was married to Sulaiman Khan (now deceased) who was a driver in the Forest Department

Ishtiaq and his wife **Razia** had three sons and six daughters, listed here from eldest to youngest.

1	Azra	Daughter. Married to a daily wager in Forest Department. Now deceased.
2	Zohra	Daughter, now deceased.
3	Rabia	Daughter. Lives in Moradabad. Married tyo Munawar Ali, mahout posted at Dhikala.
4	Asia	Daughter, married to Nayab *characut*, who is the son of Nawab Khan, mahout at Dhikala.
5	Irfan	Son, worked as *characut* in Ramnagar Forest Division.
6	Rizwan	Son, drives a tourist vehicle in Ramnagar.
7	Ghausia	Daughter, lives in Rampur.
8	Ahsan	Son, died of snakebite when he was just seven years of age.
9	Nazia	Daughter, died of shock and grief, soon after the death of her brother Ahsan.

Ishtiaq with his extended family members.

Many of Ishtiaq's elder relatives were employees in the Nawab of Rampur's elephant stables from where they ultimately came over to the Forest Department after the abolition of the Rampur state. Ishtiaq's maternal grandfather Hidayat Ali as well as his father Dulha Hasan were mahouts in the nawab's elephant stables.

The Nawab of Rampur was the owner of around 50 elephants which were housed in his *feelkhana* (elephant stable), a large building on the road to the Shahabad gate. This is why there were a huge number of mahouts, *characuts,* and other staff employed by the Nawab.

The usual entertainment for elephant owners in those days was to arrange elephant fights for their guests. This was the time when a small team of men would rile the elephants from all sides, jabbing them with long spears to get them fighting mad, and then the elephants were set on each other for a titanic contest.

Elephants being riled for a contest

Elephants lined up in Nawab Rampur's Haathi Khana in olden days

During its heydays, the Rampur state also used its elephants for *khedah* (capture of wild elephants) operations in the *terai*. Consequently, a large number of captured wild elephants used to be brought to Rampur for sale. For quite some time, Rampur remained a vibrant centre of elephant trade.

Post-independence, when the Nawab's fiefdom ended and the *feelkhana* came into disuse, it was used by the government to provide housing to the Sikh refugees who came to India after being displaced from the newly formed Pakistan. It is still called *Haathi Khana* and has provided a home to many refugee families, whose successive generations still continue to live there to this day.

CHAPTER 5

A Chronology of Life

Ishtiaq's early life was spent in Rampur, a small town in the state of Uttar Pradesh, where he lived with his parents in very modest financial circumstances. His father Dulha Hasan was a mahout working for the Forest Department, so he was usually away from Rampur, living at his place of posting. It was his wife Maseeti Begum - Ishtiaq's mother - who had the responsibility of bringing up Ishtiaq and his six siblings, consisting of three brothers and three sisters.

Ishtiaq was the third youngest of four brothers. He was never admitted to any school due to the financial constraints of the family. His education consisted only of learning to read the scriptures, for which he was sent to the house of the local *maulvi*, or Muslim cleric. These neighborhood clerics usually were as poor as the students who came to them and were themselves quite limited in the knowledge of the scriptures which they were supposed to teach. So, the teaching sessions at the *maulvi's* house usually ended in a token repetition of some verses, after which the students were made to double up as unpaid labourers, either running kitchen errands for the cleric's wife or sweeping and cleaning the house.

Ishtiaq said that he balked at the idea of being used as a servant and usually escaped from the *maulvi's* house after the token lessons. He quickly made his way to his own neighborhood, where he then spent the rest of the day loitering with his friends, either flying kites or playing the then most common game of *gulli-danda.*

These escapades went on for some time until his mother finally got wise to his bunking of the *maulvi's* classes, and loafing around with his friends. When her repeated admonishments did not have the required effect on Ishtiaq, she could bear it no longer. In desperation, she sent word to her brother Latafat Husain, who was then posted as a mahout in the Ramnagar Forest Division, about 90 km away from Rampur.

Latafat sent back word to his sister that Ishtiaq should be immediately sent to him at Ramnagar, where he would take him under his wing and see to his further upbringing. Ishtiaq told me he was not sure of the year this happened, but he does recall that when he was despatched to Ramnagar to be under his uncle Latafat's tutelage, his father was alive, but died soon after, sometime in 1950.

And so, the teenaged Ishtiaq made that journey to Ramnagar to be his maternal uncle's ward. It is evident that as a young boy, he learned everything that had to do with elephant care and management under Latafat Ali, who was a full-time mahout employed with the Forest Department. Latafat Ali also happened to be an expert in *shikar* arrangements and was much sought after by the forest department officers or their guests who were inclined towards tiger hunting.

The next three years that Ishtiaq spent with his uncle Latafat Ali at Ramnagar gave him enough knowledge about elephant care and management. It seems that a chastened Ishtiaq felt guilty about having wasted his early years in Rampur, and took it upon himself to mend his ways. He said that he worked extremely hard and tried to learn all that was taught to him by his mentor.

Three years of intense tutoring and training under Latafat Ali brought out the requisite qualities in Ishtiaq, and in 1952 he was officially made a *characut* (fodder cutter) in the Ramnagar Forest Division.

Soon after, Ishtiaq was attached to mahout Himayat Ali, who was also his maternal uncle, being the elder brother of Latafat

Ali, under whom Ishtiaq had undergone his initial tutelage. Himayat Ali was posted in the Silviculture and Working Plans Circle of the Forest Department. This attachment took Ishtiaq over a wide range of assignments ranging from Lakhimpur Kheri, Pilibhit, Ramnagar, Lansdowne, and Dehradun Forest Divisions, where Himayat Ali and his elephant were requisitioned by officers.

In 1957, Ishtiaq was posted as a *characut* in the Bahraich Forest Division. It was in 1960 during this posting that Ishtiaq was promoted as a mahout by SM Sibtain the then DFO, and was allotted his first elephant. However, this was a posting that Ishtiaq was quite averse to, and he yearned to get back to Ramnagar Forest Division where his family and friends resided. He kept hoping for the day when he could have his posting reverted to Ramnagar again.

One day, Ishtiaq got the news that one of his favourite officers RC Soni had taken charge as Chief Conservator in the state headquarters of the forest department at Lucknow. The officer knew him well, and Ishtiaq was confident that if he went in person and appealed to the Chief, he would surely favour him with a transfer back to Ramnagar.

This seemed just like a god-sent opportunity to Ishtiaq, and he wasted no time in grabbing it. He told his Range Officer that his elephant was quite ill and that he needed permission to go to the nearby township of Nanpara to fetch some medicines required for its treatment. Permission granted, Ishtiaq headed straight to Lucknow and arrived at the residence of BH Hingorani under whom Ishtiaq had worked when Hingorani was a DFO, and who was now the Chief Wildlife Warden.

Ishtiaq knew that the wives of RC Soni and BH Hingorani were close friends, and he prevailed upon Mrs Hingorani to telephone Mrs Soni to put in a word to her husband that Ishtiaq was in her house, and was desperate to seek his transfer from Bahraich to Ramnagar.

Fortified with this strong recommendation and the ladies' support, Ishtiaq went to meet the Chief Conservator, who told him that he had just taken charge, and would order his transfer soon. But Ishtiaq implored him not to send him back to Bahraich even for a single day, and the good officer gave in, and kindly ordered Ishtiaq's express transfer back to Ramnagar.

As is evident from these events, Ishtiaq had the courage of conviction that his superior officers had always been appreciative of his work during the period he had worked under them. The officers too had the kind disposition to accede to the request of an employee who may have been low-ranked, but whom they trusted and liked for the honest performance of his duties.

Relieved and happy, Ishtiaq finally ended almost three years of his posting in Bahraich, and in 1960, headed back to his favourite haunts, the Ramnagar Forest Division. This tenure now had him working in Haldwani, Ramnagar, Lansdowne, and Corbett Park for the next nine years.

In 1962 the mahout in charge of Champa elephant retired, and she was allotted to Ishtiaq. He recalls that she was one of his favourite elephants, well-trained for *shikar*, and had accompanied him on many tiger hunting trips undertaken by the forest officers of those times.

In 1965, Ishtiaq had marriage forced on him. Whenever this subject was broached by his mother, he used to evade it. His reason was that he always wanted to remain a bachelor so that he could remain unfettered in his love for the jungles. But when his mother's started weeping and grieving to make him agree to marriage, he acceded to her proposal to get married to Razia, his aunt's daughter.

In 1969, an unfortunate altercation with one of his senior officers resulted in Ishtiaq having to leave the Forest Department, and look elsewhere for a job. By now he was a married man with two children. The increased responsibilities were weighing him down, and he needed to start earning his livelihood immediately. This he did by setting up a tyre vulcanizing shop in Ramnagar.

This business went well for a few years, but later, he fell ill and had to undergo surgery for hernia. Recovering from surgery, Ishtiaq was advised by the surgeon not to lift heavy weights. This physical debility made Ishtiaq take the decision of selling off his vulcanizing shop. He then undertook some contractual work for the Irrigation Department, but could not make it a success, and suffered financial setbacks.

However, in 1978, he was re-inducted in the Forest Department with the good offices of his benefactor CB Singh, who was at that time posted as Director, Corbett Park. CB Singh had just bought two new elephants for Corbett Park and allotted one of them to Ishtiaq. After his re-induction, Ishtiaq continued to be posted in Corbett Park without a break, till the time he retired from the forest department in 2004.

Broadly enumerated, this is the chronology of events of Ishtiaq's life. The various incidents described in this book took place during that long period of 55 years, which constitutes the time frame within which his story has been woven.

CHAPTER 6

Memories of Corbett Park in Olden Times

It was quite natural that while talking about Ishtiaq's association with Ramnagar since as early as 1949, one would want to hear from him how Corbett Park in general, and Dhikala camp in particular, looked like in those olden times. Most of us who have experienced Corbett Park in the decades of the eighties, nineties and thereafter, are aware of the layout and physical features of the park as it exists now. But a historical perspective from a person who had seen the park in much earlier times would probably create an interesting imagery of days when these forests were virtually pristine, and still not damaged by the ever-increasing footfall of wildlife tourists.

I asked Ishtiaq what Corbett Park was like during the days of his earliest visits. Ishtiaq said he first came to Dhikala in 1947 as a young boy along with his father Dulha Hasan, who was a mahout in the forest department. At that time, Ishtiaq was residing with his mother in Rampur, and his father had arrived there during his transit journey from Lakhimpur to Ramnagar. Fatherly love for his young boy made Dulha Hasan accede to Ishtiaq's request to take him along on the journey to Dhikala. Before starting from Ramnagar, his father had jokingly remarked to the family members that they were actually going to '*Kala Pani*' - a place of exile, so remote was the location of Dhikala considered to be during those early days. There was no tourist activity at Dhikala, and only forest officers used to go there by animal transport in the course of duty.

On that trip, the Working Plan Conservator's caravan comprised two elephants and six camels. The camp paraphernalia was transported by the camels while the officers were mounted on elephants. The other staff in the retinue had to walk the distance of about 50 km from Ramnagar to Dhikala. The young Ishtiaq rode on the elephant his father was driving. The DFO was allotted one elephant and two camels, while the Ranger was given one horse for transportation.

Reaching Dhikala they all slept in the tents pitched around the old forest rest house, while the officers and camp clerks occupied the rest house. When Ishtiaq got out of his tent early the next morning, he saw what seemed like hundreds of cattle horns in the grassland all around. He ruefully remarked to his father, "Why did you say there is no habitation here? Look at all these cattle grazing around." His father then told him that these were actually wild animals and that there were no villages there.

So Ishtiaq climbed up on a vantage point to see vast herds of herbivores. He remarked that such a rich spot would be a great attraction for hunters. But his father explained that this place was a no-hunting zone named after Governor Hailey who had come here for *shikar* but was so struck by the beauty of the place and the bountiful wildlife present there, that he ordered a complete ban on hunting in the area.

The next trip Ishtiaq made to Dhikala was with Conservator GM Hopkins who was touring the area while preparing the Working Plan. Elaborating on the constitution of the Conservator's camp he said the staff consisted of two orderlies, one bearer, one jamadar, one cook for the Conservator, one camp clerk, one khalasi for the camp clerk, and one *dak* (mail) runner. The mail runners did their trip on foot, and the mail used to be carried daily in relays from Ramnagar to Dhangadhi, Dhangadhi to Sarpaduli, and from Sarpaduli to Dhikala.

Preparation of Working Plans was a fairly long-drawn work, extending to months of studying and detailing the existing forest wealth (land, flora, fauna & water resources) including climatic and biotic factors of the area. Based on those detailed documents, the management practices were outlined for the conservation, preservation, and efficient utilization of these forest resources. Working Plans were chiefly the responsibility of Divisional Forest Officer, Working Plan Officer, and the Conservator of Forests.

At that time Dhikala camp only had the still-existing old FRH with four rooms, along with a kitchen and some separate living quarters for the mahouts and staff posted there. There was the *feelkhana* and stables to house the forest department elephants and other animals used in those days for transportation.

The entire area underlying Dhikala was a good forest belt resplendent with *sheesham* trees. Interspersed among these forests were undulating grasslands on both sides of the Ramganga river. Wildlife was so dense around the camp that one could see a sea of antlers sticking out from the grasslands on all sides of the camp. Naturally, the herbivores were trailed by predators, and the air was filled with alarm calls both at night and day.

The Ramganga at that time did not flow as close to Dhikala camp as it does now. The main river used to run a winding course somewhere in the middle of the forests lying between Dhikala and Phulai Sot located on the ridge to the north of Dhikala. Its banks were also lined with rows and rows of *sheesham bojhis* or stands.

There used to be crocodiles, *mahseer* (Genus *Tor*), and a large variety of other fish in the waters of the Ramganga and the Sonanadi. Later, when the Kalagarh dam created the reservoir on the Ramganga, the still waters became the habitat for goonch (a catfish of genus *Bugarius*). These proliferated and attained huge sizes. Being carnivorous, they did considerable damage to populations of other fish by preying on their fry and fingerlings.

Dhikala FRH as it used to be in olden times

Dhikala FRH as it is now

The forests were home to any number of elephants, tigers, panthers, bears, antelope, deer, and pigs. Birds were equally numerous, and they added beauty, colour and song to the place.

There used to be a path that started from near the north-western edge of Dhikala camp and went straight to Kanda road crossing the *chaurs,* and the Ramganga by a wooden bridge. That path ceased to exist after the inundation brought on by the construction of the Kalagarh dam.

Apart from the Dhikala camp, there were Bhoksar and Hathikund camps. Whereas the Bhoksar area is now completely submerged under the water body created by the Kalagarh dam, the remains of Hathikund can still be seen, since it was located on higher ground.

I wanted to know more about Bhoksar, since I remember reading somewhere that it always had a dense population of pythons. Ishtiaq told me that Bhoksar was a well-developed forest establishment with a rest house, a small medical facility for staff, sprawling gardens, *chaurs* or grasslands all around, and a large pool nearby which was called Naka Tal. It was named thus because it had a thriving population of gharial (*Gavialis gangeticus*), locally called 'naka' because of the protuberances on the upper portion of its snout. As for pythons, Ishtiaq confirmed that it was quite usual to see 18-footer pythons in that area.

An interesting piece of information provided by Ishtiaq about Bhoksar was that gold was present in the Sonanadi river running through the area. The Sonanadi is an important tributary of the Ramganga and enters the park from the northwest direction to meet the Ramganga at the reservoir formed by the submergence of the forests after the Kalagarh Dam was built.

The name 'Sonanadi' means 'river of gold'. In older times particles of gold were found in the alluvial deposits washed down from the higher areas. This precious metal used to be regularly extracted from the sandy bed of the river through the simple procedure of sieving and washing.

The local inhabitants of that area were called Bhokse, and they used to be employed by the government contractor to pan the river for gold dust. The contractor used to pay them based on the weight of gold dust each had collected. The dust was then taken to the market in Kashipur where it was smelted and converted into ornamental gold.

I wanted to know about the continuity between the forest ranges of Nainital and Dehradun before the Kalagarh dam was built. The idea was to find out if there was an unrestricted movement of wild elephants between the two ranges, and whether the construction of the dam had broken off the elephant corridor and restricted the gene pool of elephant populations living in both ranges.

 Ishtiaq said that the dam did pose a hindrance to the migration route of elephants, but he also confirmed that elephants still managed to cross over from Corbett Park to Rajaji Park by the existing forest routes. It was only the dense human settlement in the Kalagarh area which effectively blocked their traditional route from olden times.

However, the elephants now use the new corridor which spans Rathuadhab in Corbett Park to Phool Chaur near Kotdwar, then to Laldhang, and from there to Chilla in Rajaji Park. I concede that various scientific studies on this issue must have dwelt at length about the pros and cons of projects like the Kalagarh dam, but my attempt was only to gauge what local wisdom had to say about these 'pompously' scientific issues.

 The advantages or disadvantages of the Kalagarh dam can be discussed ad infinitum, but it is generally felt that it greatly damaged the forest ecosystem of Corbett Park. The stagnating waters of Ramganga reservoir around the park have created a huge area where trees have all died and swamp areas have been created over vast expanses that earlier used to be thick forests. Consequently, a huge amount of forest timber belonging to those dead trees had gone waste, without any future chance of reforestation of that area.

I understand that Ishtiaq is not expected to comprehend the science of ecosystems that forbids the removal of any fallen tree from the forest floor since it constitutes the habitat of huge biodiversity. But he goes on to further lament that in Dhikala, the adverse effect on animals due to the submergence was quite evident since their grazing area had been reduced. The grasses in the *chaurs* remain unmanaged, thus becoming coarse and unpalatable to herbivores. This is why the density of herbivorous around Dhikala had reduced as compared to olden times. With the scarcity of herbivores, the predators too had been in decline. Although tiger numbers increased elsewhere in Corbett Park, Dhikala suffered a decline in tiger presence.

Ishtiaq recalled that after this trip in 1952, he was transferred to Bahraich forest division in 1957 from where he was able to have himself transferred back to Ramnagar in 1960. After staying for two years in the Ramnagar forest division, he was given marching orders in 1962 to proceed to Lansdowne to join the team of forest department engaged in the preparation of the Lansdowne Working Plan.

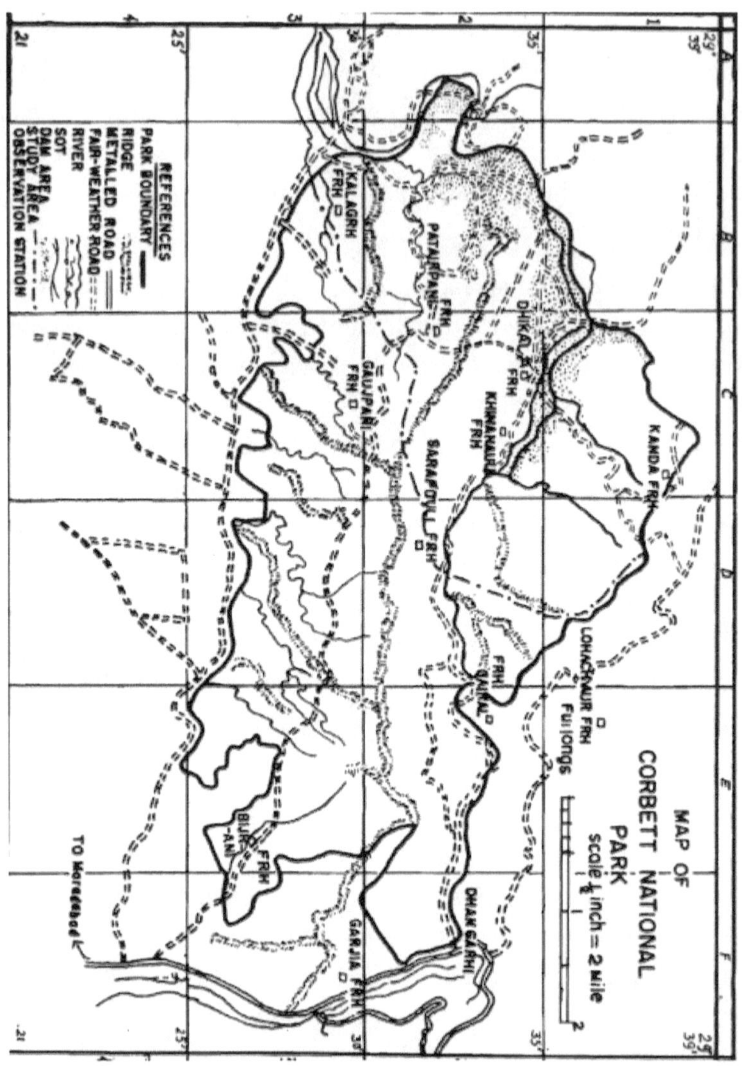

A general layout map of Corbett Tiger Reserve

CHAPTER 7

Skirmishes with Dacoits

Considering that Ishtiaq spent almost his entire life working in the forests of undivided Uttar Pradesh, it is no wonder that he was also destined to come face to face with bandits and brigands, for whom the jungles were much-favoured haunts since they provided them with a haven to hide and evade capture by the police. Ishtiaq recounts his encounter with a dacoit named Basheera, which occurred in 1952 when he was posted at Lalkuan in the Haldwani forest division as a *characut* under mahout Himayat Ali.

Urgent orders were received that Himayat Ali and his elephant immediately report at Dudhwa, where the Lakhimpur Kheri Working Plan was being conducted by Conservator GM Hopkins and DFO Bhatia. From Lalkuan, the mahout and his elephant embarked upon the 100 odd mile journey. Himayat Ali was accompanied by Ishtiaq and another *characut*. Arriving at Lakhimpur after the arduous week-long journey, they promptly got down to performing their assigned duties for the next two months.

With the onset of rains, the Conservator's camp was wound up and they all started the return journey to their base, Lalkuan. Ishtiaq recalls that it was somewhere near Puranpur that they had made a stop to rest the elephant for the night. This was an area where the dacoit Basheera was known to be active. In the afternoon, Ishtiaq rode the elephant into the forests to cut its fodder for the night.

Having gone some distance, he was suddenly accosted by two desperate-looking characters, who held him up at gunpoint and ordered him to make the elephant sit down so that they could climb aboard. Being quite scared of them, Ishtiaq complied with alacrity and made the elephant kneel, to enable them to come up onto the elephant's pad.

The first thing they did was to take possession of Ishtiaq's axe, used by him for lopping fodder. Thereafter, they ordered Ishtiaq to take them around the forest so that they could shoot a chital for the pot. It was only after about two hours that they could finally manage to shoot one. But Ishtiaq's ordeal was not over yet. The desperadoes now made him skin the chital, cut the venison into pieces, and pack it in a gunny bag.

It was only when he was through with this back-breaking job, that the two men finally took hold of the gunny bag and quickly made their way into the forest. A terribly shaken Ishtiaq was fully convinced that he had surely had a run-in with Basheera, and kept thanking his stars that he had come out none the worse for the experience.

In answer to my question about how he could have been so positive about the identification of Basheera, Ishtiaq points out that before they freed him, the dacoits gave back possession of his axe to him. This, according to him, could only have been done by Basheera, who had the reputation of being a '*ghareeb parvar*' - a sort of Robin Hood character who was never known to loot or harm the poor.

But it does seem that the poor elephant was surely put to some discomfort, since the whole incident had gone on till late evening and Ishtiaq, even with his axe regained, had the singular thought of beating a hasty retreat to the safety of the camp and did not stop to cut green fodder to feed the elephant during the night.

Ishtiaq sums up this story by saying that a couple of years later, the exploits of Basheera ended when he was shot dead. Subsequently, his wife - known to be a crack shot herself - took over the dacoit gang for a while before being captured by the police and put in prison, where she gave birth to a child.

In another incident that took place in 1959, Ishtiaq had an encounter with another dacoit gang. This time he was posted in the Motipur range of the Bahraich forest division. Since his living quarters were next to the Deputy Ranger's house, he was often invited to the officer's house for evening tea and snacks.

He recalls that one day some guests arrived at the Deputy Ranger's house when the officer was away for a few days. To prepare lunch for the guests, the Deputy Ranger's wife handed Ishtiaq her husband's shotgun and requested him to shoot some jungle fowl for the pot. Having shot a couple, Ishtiaq handed over the birds to the kitchen staff and sat down in front of his shack to clean the gun before returning it to the officer's house.

Late that night while he slept in the open, he was roughly woken up by someone smothering him. As he came to his senses, he found three men leaning over him, two of whom had their spears to his neck while the third had a gun on his head. They threateningly ordered him to hand over the gun to them. "But I don't have a gun," Ishtiaq told them. "Don't lie," one of them hissed, and slapped him. "We saw you cleaning it in the evening." Even in the face of this grave threat, Ishtiaq had the presence of mind not to tell the truth, since he knew that the Deputy Ranger was not at home, and only his wife and daughter were alone in the house. Fearing that they might come to harm if the dacoits went in there, Ishtiaq promptly lied to them that the gun was in the Ranger's house.

Since the Ranger was present and there were other men sleeping in his compound, the dacoits evidently were not prepared to risk an encounter with them. Cautioning Ishtiaq not to tell anyone of their coming, they left him and quietly slipped off into the jungle.

Although Ishtiaq never mentioned it to anyone, it seems that his *characut* had woken up in the night while this episode was going on. He let out the secret of the dacoits' intrusion to the game guard, who went and mentioned it to the *Pradhan* or the village headman. From there the news filtered to the police picket stationed at the nearby village.

During the day, a constable came over to the range office to tell Ishtiaq that he was being summoned by the Police Inspector to record details of what had happened in the night. Apprehensive about the dacoits' warning, Ishtiaq flatly denied anything of that sort having happened. He also refused to go with the constable on the plea that he would not be able to come to the village without the permission of his superiors, who were not present there at that moment. The constable left but soon returned with the Inspector who started asking investigative questions. Ishtiaq again denied that any such incident had taken place.

The irritated Police Inspector angrily backtracked on the chain of informants. The Pradhan said it was the game guard who told him, and the game guard said it was the *characut* who told him. The cornered *characut* got out of the situation by angrily accosting the game guard and demanding whether he would believe anything told to him by someone who was in a state of inebriation. Ishtiaq admits that it was the *characut*'s ingenuity that saved the day, since the policemen believed him and dropped the matter there.

A few days later, Ishtiaq was out in the forests on his elephant when he was confronted by three strangers, who ordered him to get off the elephant and accompany them. Ishtiaq tried to persuade them to let him go, saying the elephant would stray into deep forests if left by itself. But they would have none of his arguments and made him chain the elephant to a tree. After walking for some time, they blindfolded him and told him that he was being taken to their 'sardar' or leader.

By now Ishtiaq had no doubt in his mind that he was in the hands of dacoits, and started becoming apprehensive about their intentions. But it was reassuring to notice that they were not acting with belligerence or roughness, but were handling him gently on the way. After walking like that for some time, they stopped and took off his blindfold.

The scene that confronted him was clearly that of a makeshift camp, with some rough-looking characters lolling around. The gang leader, before whom he was made to stand, addressed Ishtiaq mockingly. "So, you went ahead and informed the police even though I had told you not to?" he asked. Backed with the confidence that he had not done so, Ishtiaq pleadingly told him that he was not guilty on that count.

The gang leader was quick to acquiesce and admitted that he was only joking since he knew that Ishtiaq was speaking the truth. He then went on to speak in a condescending tone and told Ishtiaq that since the gang was on the run, they were running short of rations. Would it be possible for Ishtiaq to supply them with some? To this Ishtiaq answered truthfully that he was quite broke, not having received his salary for the past three months.

The dacoit leader then told him that he would have to provide them with some cigarettes at least. It was decided that Ishtiaq would go to the nearby village of Mihipurwa to get a stock of Scissors brand of cigarettes and a pack of matchboxes. Two of the gang members would accompany him to keep an eye on him and see that he did not speak to anyone in the village.

Ishtiaq himself was now in a quandary since he did not have any money to buy the cigarette and matches. So he went over to a clothes shop owner called Saifu, who he happened to know. He told Saifu that he was in a predicament, that he had to buy a stock of cigarettes and matches for one of his superiors, but had unfortunately run out of money at the moment. Could Saifu help him buy these items, for which he would pay as soon as he got his next salary? The good man Saifu was forthcoming in his help and very soon, Ishtiaq was triumphantly headed back for the dacoit hideout, again blindfolded and escorted by his two guards.

As soon as he entered the bandit hideout, he heard the leader shouting angrily at Ishtiaq's escorts, demanding why they had blindfolded him. He told them that there was no need for such measures since Ishtiaq was now his 'trustworthy friend'. Thanking Ishtiaq for the stuff that he had brought, the dacoit leader also pointedly announced that they were shifting camp that very moment, thereby making it clear to Ishtiaq that any information about this camp would cease to have importance or relevance for the police.

But, Ishtiaq says that he never did harbour any intentions of involving the police in this incident, and was only relieved and happy that he was allowed to go home without any serious injury or loss.

The encounters that Ishtiaq had with dacoits outline the fact that in those days dacoits and forest brigands always held the officers and staff of the forest department in high esteem. This could stem from their understanding that since forests were their only safe havens from the law, they would do well not to annoy or antagonize the people of the forest department.

This brings to mind the reminiscences written by a retired Deputy Conservator Keshwa Nand about his own encounter with dacoits during his service period in the 1920s to 1940s. These reminiscences also underline the tacit honour and esteem accorded to forest officers by dacoits. Here, the dacoit encountered by Keshwa Nand was none other than the celebrated Sultana *Daku* – who even finds mention in the books of Jim Corbett.

In the UP Forest Department Souvenir issued in 1961, Keshwa Nand *writes "I am writing down this small article with the hope that it would give an inkling of the conditions that obtained in our forests. I actually started my practical training in the year 1914 and underwent the Rangers' Course of 1915-17. The roads which were used by DFO's and District Officers for inspection and general tours inside the jungles as well as villages dotted about in the forests were in very bad state of repairs for the greater part of the year. The forests were so l;onely and forsaken that outlaws, dacoits and bad characters found it very easy to make forests their hiding places and carry out their nefarious activities from there.*

The conditions existing at that time can be illustrated by the following account that I am giving in brief of two dacoits who were a terror to the population living in the villages. There was one Kadere Khan operating in the forests of the Bijnor district and the adjoining forests in the bhabar portion of the Garhwal district. This desperado used to go about alone with a sword hanging down his waist and a gun slung across his shoulder. He was a very atrocious and fearless man. During his rounds when he used to go about collecting money from villagers which he called his tribute, he often asked villagers to tell him whose reign it was. If the fellow replied saying that it was Kadere Khan's reign, he was spared but if anyone hesitated and did not acknowledge his reign, he was more often than not shot dead on the spot.

But strangely enough Kadere Khan was also a respectful man who held in high esteem all the local forest officials. He was particularly courteous to a local officer in-charge who had his jurisdiction from Sarda to Ganga as a Girdawar Ranger (Girdawar meaning "supervising" as opposed to "Revenue" Ranger). To this official, Kadere Khan used to send, by way of homage, basketfuls of sweets on Diwali festival, the courier taking 2-3 days to reach the village of the Forest Office. Such were the times in the past history of forests.

This may appear incredible to the younger generation, but it was all a fact. I am narrating one more story of those by gone days. It is based on my own personal experience and not on hearsay. It was about 1922 and relates to a desperate dacoit, Sultana by name, who was a terror for the country where he operated. His depredations extended over the country stretching along the foot hills from the river Sarda in the east to the Yamuna in the west. He was seldom known to go beyond the Sarda and the Yamuna.

In his last days just before his downfall, his plunder of the Timli village in Dehra Dun district was a sensational event. His modus operandi was very daring. He with his gang used to get into a village for plundering and looting soon after dusk because at that time the doors in the houses would still remain open and there would not be enough light to recognise the intruders. His active gang consisted of about 40 men, he also had an astrologer-pandit in the gang who used to decide upon favourable time for an "operation" and also performed puja afterwards to seek divine pardon for the brutalities committed by the dacoits during an "operation".

This gang of Sultana had somehow attained such a great notoriety that it could easily defy the authority of the local custodians of law and order with impunity. The local district armed police which used to patrol the forest areas from time to time was never courageous enough to approach the likely places of the dacoits' shifting abodes. The force and strength of the gang was considered to be too great.

But later when the depredations of the Sultana gang grew out of proportion, a special unit of armed police was set up under the command of Young of the Indian Police to liquidate the dacoit gang. Young had at least 2 deputy Superintendents and several Inspectors and Sub Inspectors of Police to help him besides the corps of constables.

But when Sultana was at the zenith of his power and notoriety, I came across him several times during the course of my inspections of the forests. For the first time I met him on the 13th of February in the year 1922 or 1923, the exact year has just now slipped from my memory, at a place called Nawabkund in the Jaspur Range of Ramnagar Forest Division.

The spot was about 3 miles to the south-west of the Maldhan Forest Rest House. At this meeting, Sultana who was a terror to the locality, behaved as a gentleman and during the course of our talk he said, to quote his own words, "Hum to huzur ki jootiyon ki khak hain" (We are the dust of your shoes). He had that sort of sentiment for the forest people.

My own conscience also dictated me to act similarly and so I picked up the money but kept it separately wrapped up in a piece of paper. When, later on, I came to Dehra Dun on leave, I gave away these coins to an old destitute woman. I thought the tainted money could thus, go down for a better purpose.

Jim Corbett (L) & Freddy Young (C) take a break while on Sultana's trail.

Sultana after his capture.

I came across Sultana again and again several times. He was always very courteous towards me. For most of the time Sultana with his gang stayed in the forests of Jaspur Range. It was a convenient spot for him both for his "operations" as well as for the disposal of the booty in the markets of Kashipur and Jaspur.

The dramas enacted by Kadere Khan and Sultana within the forests, merely illustrate the dreadful conditions which prevailed in the forests of Uttar Pradesh in those hoary years of the past. Vast stretches of dense forests were rendered totally unfathomable for utter lack of means of communications. Time and law had very little sway within the bosom of the forest, which befriended with all manner of ferocity both of men and denizens and offered a ready home for them to thrive upon.

But the older generations of foresters then knew no better and had to contend with those bleak conditions with a good deal more of courage and caution than what the present generation of foresters would deem really "necessary" today!"

I have taken recourse to quoting Keshwa Nand's experiences to buttress Ishtiaq's narrative. With this excerpt from a venerable forest officer, I put *'finis'* to Ishtiaq's account of his skirmishes with dacoits.

CHAPTER 8

Days of Tiger Shikar

I now asked Ishtiaq about the tiger *shikar* that he had been associated with when his superior officers or their guests went on these hunting trips.

It should be understood here that those were times when tiger hunting was the order of the day and not an abomination that it became in later years. There can be no debate here on the merits or demerits of *shikar*, but since tiger-hunting happened to be an integral part of Ishtiaq's life and times, it has to find mention in his story.

Ishtiaq's eyes light up with these memories. This is where he comes into his own as an expert mahout who could control his elephant so steadily that the hunter occupying the howdah behind him is placed in a vantage position, and is able to squeeze off that accurate shot which brings down the angry, charging tiger. And he impresses upon us in no uncertain terms, that it was this prowess that made him a most sought-after and favoured mahout all through the duration of his service in the forest department.

As long as Ishtiaq worked in the Working Plan, Conservator BP Srivastava - a keen *shikari* himself - and other *shikari* officers always used to requisition his services for their hunting trips. Coupled with Ishtiaq's own prowess as a mahout was his elephant Champa, who was a most steady and dependable elephant for tiger hunting.

Champa was allotted to Ishtiaq in 1962 and remained his long-standing companion for seven years. During the time that she was under his charge in the Haldwani Forest Division, she had also given birth to a calf. Later, she was transferred from her duties in the Working Plan to Corbett Park where she was stationed at Bijrani FRH as a safari elephant till the time she died when she had attained the age of about 70 to 75 years.

With the mention of Conservator BP Srivastava as a passionate and keen *shikari*, it would also be pertinent to know some more about what the long-serving officer had to say on the subject of *shikar*. It should be kept in mind that the following views expressed by him, date back to the 1960s while he was still serving in the forest department.

In the *UP Forest Department Souvenir* issued in 1961, BP Srivastava writes, "*With the great political changes that have taken place in the country and the replacement of the British rule by a democratic Government of the people, the pattern of shikar and the type of people who indulge in it have also undergone considerable changes.*

In the days of British rule, shikar, at least on any considerable scale, was almost the complete preserve of British officers (with a small sprinkling of Indian officers), the Rajas, the Maharajas, the Taluqdars and Zamindars. Many of the latter owned forests of their own, which they jealously guarded as game preserves. The great awe in which Government and Government officials were held resulted in a stricter protection of the Government forests against poaching, with the consequence that in spite of a large number of animals shot every year the animal population remained more or less constant.

Almost every Forest Officer was a keen shikari and naturalist. In fact, every new entrant to the service was encouraged to take up this hobby, and those who didn't were looked down upon. Though no such clause existed in the service rules, it was an unwritten tradition that no ACF was considered fit to hold charge of a division unless he had shot a tiger. Such an atmosphere developed a breed of Forest Officers who guarded the wild life as jealously as they did the forest trees. Infringement of game rules was seriously taken, and dealt with a strong hand.

With the advent of Independence and the abolition of Indian States and Zamindari system, the strictly protected game preserves of the Rajas and Zamindars lost their sanctity, and untold damage was done to the animals existing in them.

Hundreds and thousands of deer, antelope and pigs were slaughtered from jeeps and other moving vehicles during the course of a few years. In the reserved forests as well, poaching and indiscriminate shooting became rampant. The Forest Guard and the Forest Ranger were no more the demi-gods they used to be in the old days.

Public opinion, however, soon raised its voice against the rapid disappearance of our very valuable forest heritage, and Government machinery started to move slowly but steadily. In the United Provinces a Game Preservation Circle (which was subsequently reorganised as a division) was formed in 1956 and some other states also followed suit.

Methods of shikar, and by shikar is mainly implied the shooting of tigers, have not undergone much change. Even now, as before, the recognised methods of shooting tigers are by a beat with elephants, or from a machan over a dead or live bait, or stalking from the back of an elephant or on foot. The only notable change, however, is that the number of elephants used for beating is considerably less than in the old days.

The reason is not far to seek. With the abolition of the erstwhile princely States and the Zamindari system, and as a sequel to rising prices, very few elephants are maintained. It becomes difficult now to collect even half a dozen elephants for a beat, whereas in the old days four times the number could be easily collected for a tiger beat.

During the nineteenth century the Commissariat Department as it was then called, maintained a large stable of elephants at Bareilly, and it was possible to hire them for shooting parties. The Nawab of Rampur was said to maintain a stable of 50 elephants.

Beaters' wages have also risen so much so that the number of beaters employed for beats is nowhere so large as it used to be. Where 200 beaters for a beat used to be the normal figure, it is difficult, ordinarily, to collect or afford even 20 today.

The consequence has been that beats have become less frequent and when held, less effective in bringing a tiger to the bag. As a result of this, more attempts are now made at shooting tigers from a machan than formerly. By far the most interesting and sporting way of shooting tigers and other game by Forest Officers is to stalk and shoot them from elephant-back. Sport can thus be combined with work, and lonely evenings in the forests can be turned to advantage.

Tigers and illicit fellings are seldom found within easy reach of motor roads. A Forest Officer who is keen on observing nature and makes it a point to go out in the forests every morning or evening either on elephant or on foot with a rifle in hand, learns much about forestry that he would otherwise seldom have an opportunity to do. The fact that he is liable to visit the most unfrequented parts of the forests at any time has a salutary effect on forest conservation in general".

Having taken care of this little introduction on Conservator BP Srivastava's personal opinion on the subject of *shikar* vis-a-vis a forest officer's job, I now return to Ishtiaq's narrative.

The Tigress of Lalkuan

Ishtiaq recounted witnessing a tigress attacking an old woman during the time he was posted in Lalkuan. He had been out on an early morning ride with his elephant to fetch its ration of sugarcane when he heard the angry snarl of a tigress lying somewhere in the scrub forest bordering the forest road. The snarl was directed at an old woman who was walking on the forest path with a head-load of firewood. As was later found out, this old woman happened to be stone-deaf. The tigress had snarled at the woman probably trying to warn her away from the place where she lay nursing her cubs. Unable to hear the tigress' warning, she kept on approaching the spot where the tigress lay.

Ishtiaq could gauge the situation, but he was still some distance away from the woman. He shouted and gesticulated at her, and tried to rush his elephant towards the woman to save her. But in an instant, the tigress was out charging at the woman. She reared up on her hind legs and lashed out at the woman's face, dropping her in an instant. She then clamped her canines in the woman's throat, shook her vigorously, and dragged her into the forest. All this happened so quickly that Ishtiaq's presence or his yelling had no effect on the tigress.

When Ishtiaq gave news of this attack to BP Srivastava, who was then the Conservator, Haldwani Working Plan, he ordered his staff to locate the spot where the tigress had taken the dead woman, and build a machan over it. He himself proceeded from Haldwani to shoot the tigress. Those were times when forest officers could shoot aberrant tigers for the safety of local inhabitants. And this tigress had just killed a woman, albeit after giving ample warning to the woman against entering her domain.

By the time BP Srivastava arrived at the site, his staff had made all the arrangements. The machan had been built and an elephant and mahout were ready at his disposal. He climbed into the machan at about 4 PM and by 4.45 PM the shot had been taken, ending the tigress' short-lived career as a man-killer. As mentioned by Ishtiaq earlier, BP Srivastava was known in the department as a keen *shikari*, and had wasted no time in undertaking the responsibility of eliminating the tigress, which could otherwise have become a potential threat to the local inhabitants.

One only wonders sadly that if the tigress was a nursing mother, and had killed the woman in defence of her cubs, what happened to them after their mother was killed. Ishtiaq had no recollection of their fate. Well, it can only be hoped that a good forest officer like BP Srivastava must certainly have taken some proactive measure regarding the little ones.

The Botched Shikar at Jaulasal

One incident concerning a near-botched tiger *shikar* that BP Srivastava was fond of recounting was the one about EA Smythies and his wife Olive. Smythies was a Conservator in the Forest Service till around 1940 and was also posted as DFO Ramnagar during 1917-18. His association with Jim Corbett is well-documented, and together with Corbett, he did some pioneering work in the establishment of the Hailey National Park which later was renamed as Corbett Park. This *shikar* incident took place in Jaulasal (now in Nandhaur wildlife sanctuary located in Haldwani forest division) sometime in 1937. The Smythies were both great *shikaris*, and when a tiger's natural kill near Jaulasal FRH presented them with a chance to bag the tiger, they went for it. Two machans were separately built over the kill site, one for each. Both ascended their respective machans in the afternoon to await the tiger's arrival.

The tiger came before the sun had set, and started eating from the kill. Olive took the first shot at the tiger but failed to kill it.

The injured tiger rushed snarling at her tree and was able to climb it almost to the level of the machan, angrily trying to claw at the lady in it. On the other machan, EA Smythies fumbled to fire but lost his balance and all his cartridges fell to the ground. He now had just one in the rifle chamber.

In the other machan, Olive put her weapon almost into the tiger's mouth and pulled the trigger, but she had a misfire. In the melee, she fell off from the machan while the tiger still hung on to it. EA Smythies now fired his only remaining bullet at the tiger and dropped him dead.

If one goes to Jaulasal FRH today, one would find a pillar built in commemoration of the bravery displayed by the Smythies. There is also a little museum there, where I saw photographs of EA Smythies, FW Champion, and other forest officers who served there in those olden times. A small sit-out area under the 14-foot pillar is a great spot to spend some quiet time in those lovely forests of Jaulasal.

Conservator GM Hopkins' Shikar

GM Hopkins was Conservator, Working Plans and Research Circle, United Provinces. Ishtiaq came in contact with him when he was posted as a *characut* with his uncle Himayat Ali mahout who was serving under Hopkins. Ishtiaq recalls his visit to Corbett Park in 1952 when he went along with the entourage of Hopkins. Their camp was established in the Bhoksar area.

A local herder had kept a few cows there for supplying milk to the staff at Bhoksar. One afternoon, while Hopkins was having his siesta, the herder came running into camp to inform that one of his milch cows had been killed by a tiger. He went on to say that the tiger was now lying up with the dead cow in the grassland around the camp area. He requested the staff to wake up the Conservator *sahib*, so he could shoot the tiger. Ishtiaq thought that considering the sparseness of cover in the grassland, it was hard to believe that a tiger could have been hidden in there. So, he asked the herdsman to first show them the tiger before they woke up the sleeping *sahib.*

They walked on guided by the herdsman and saw a lone *khair* tree standing amidst the grassland with a small patch of lantana around it. Under the *khair* tree, they could now just make out the bright white colour of the cow and the tiger feeding on it. They slowly retraced their way back to camp so as not to disturb the feeding tiger. Fortified by the clear evidence of the tiger's presence, they now informed Hopkins who ordered them to get the elephant ready. He also ordered that the herdsman also accompany them on the elephant.

Reaching the spot, the tiger was sighted feeding on the cow's carcass. Directing Ishtiaq to hold the elephant steady, Hopkins called out to his orderly sitting behind him, "*Fakeer Singh, rifle do*". Fakeer Singh promptly handed the weapon to Hopkins. He raised it and took careful aim at the tiger, but handed it back to Fakeer Singh and called for the .12 bore shotgun. The orderly handed the shotgun to him as ordered. This time too, Hopkins aimed but did not fire. He now ordered the herdsman to get down from the elephant, gather a few stones, and then get back on the elephant.

Once that was done, Hopkins asked the herdsman to throw the stones at the tiger and make him run. Seeing all this, a perplexed and taciturn Ishtiaq thought to himself, "*Yeh tayger maar riya hai ki bhaga riya hai?*" (Has he come to shoot the tiger or chase it away?).

As the herdsman's stones fell around him, the tiger left the cow and started running away, fully visible in the short grass. Once again came the terse order, "*Faqeer Singh, rifle do.*"

One snapshot later, the running tiger turned a few somersaults, dropping dead with his face now facing in the opposite direction. It was then that Ishtiaq smilingly revealed that he came to know later that Hopkins was a crack shot, which was why shooting a sitting tiger at close range was anathema to him.

In another *shikar* episode at Chilla, Ishtiaq said that a tiger was being beaten on his kill and suddenly charged towards the line of elephants beating for him. A couple of elephants broke ranks and ran helter-skelter away from the charging tiger. Hopkins was on his elephant with his rifle ready. He motioned to the remaining mahouts to drive the tiger his way, muttering that he would shoot the tiger in the eye. Ishtiaq says that true to his word, the bullet pierced the tiger's eye so cleanly that "*uski palak tak nahi kati thi*" (not even the eyelids were cut).

The VIP Shikaris

I asked Ishtiaq about the VIP *shikaris* in whose retinue he had the opportunity to play an active role. He said that as long as he served under Conservator BP Srivastava, there was a stream of officers and guests coming over for tiger *shikar*, of which he was always a part. But the two important *shikaris* that came to his mind were Maharajkumar of Vizianagram (Vizzy), and General Thimayya of the Indian Army. He recalled that he assisted twice in *shikar* arrangements for Vizzy, and twice for the General.

To the question about where these *shikars* were carried out, Ishtiaq said that for Vizzy, the first one was organized in a place called Gaurikhera, about 6 km from Lalkuan. Gaurikhera lay somewhere near the junction of the road from where one could go either in the direction of Sitarganj on one side, or Khatima on the other. The second *shikar* in which Ishtiaq assisted Vizzy was arranged in 1965 near Hathikund in Corbett Park. Hathikund used to be a great wildlife habitat at that time but now lies submerged under the waters of the reservoir created by the Kalagarh dam.

Vizzy was 'royalty' so I wanted to know if the royals and old-time British officers used ornate and elaborate howdahs during their *shikar*. But Ishtiaq said that the officers used the same simple howdahs as are being used at present. It was only the rajas and nawabs who used elaborate howdahs, replete with canopy and decorations. Their servant would be seated at the back, outside the howdah. From there he would hand over to his master whatever he called for, be it the weapon or the all-important bottle in which the royal urine was discharged by the howdah's occupant. The bottle would then be handed back to the servant, who would discreetly empty the contents and then keep it ready till the next time that the royal bladder bloated again.

Ishtiaq recalled that during *shikar*, Vizzy hardly spoke a word, but all his commands were through silent gestures to his orderly. He went on to narrate the tale when Vizzy fell off his elephant during one *shikar*, after a wounded tiger charged back at the line of elephants, sending them running in all directions. Vizzy fell backward from his howdah, landed on the rear-end of the elephant's back, then slipped down and fell heavily to the ground. This fall led to his sustained debility, and also marked the end of his hunting days. He was under prolonged treatment and later died in December 1965.

General Thimayya was the other VIP guest whose *shikar* retinue Ishtiaq was a part of. He recalls the General as being a very tall man, but he did not have any sternness in his countenance. He was quite jovial and excited during the times he was on the trail of the tigers he hunted. The two *shikars* of the General that Ishtiaq took part in, were organized at Powalgarh and Sitabani.

Recounting the one at Sitabani, Ishtiaq said that the Tedha block in Sitabani was a rich one for tiger shooting. The General was a guest of a local landlord named Belwal. During the course of Belwal's arrangement for the mahouts, there had been some altercation between the mahouts and the host. As an outcome of this grudge, the mahouts had purposely let the tiger escape from the beat, with the result that the General kept sitting on the machan waiting for the tiger but since it had already been allowed by the 'stops' to break free, the General could only draw a blank.

In the evening the General expressed his resentment to Belwal about the shoddily arranged beat. Belwal understood that the mahouts had done so to teach him a lesson by embarrassing him in the eyes of his valued guest. So Belwal beseeched the General to address the mahouts himself, and motivate them to perform better in the next beat on the morrow.

The mahouts were all called over to assemble at Belwal's house, where the General addressed them politely and exhorted them to be on their top performance the next day. The mahouts were suitably impressed by the General's address and decided amongst themselves that the wishes of the great army man would be fulfilled. They also decided that all the mahouts would act as 'stops' during the beat to ensure that the tiger could not slip through. Further, in their places, all the elephants bringing up the beat would be manned by the *characuts*.

The block which had to be beaten was a rectangular one. All the mahouts climbed on trees on both the long sides of the block, the machan was placed on the shorter side, while the remaining side was the one from where the line of elephants and the beaters would start moving noisily into the block, funnelling the tiger towards the machan on which the General sat.

The beat got off to a start, and the noisy beaters started making their way towards the machan. It disturbed the tiger lying somewhere in the line of the beat, and he started moving unhurriedly towards the machan, stopping now and then to look back at the sound of the beaters approaching towards him. As he came near the machan, he stopped and sat on his haunches, still looking back.

The General raised his rifle and shot the tiger, which rolled over and died. The sound of the shot had barely died down when a pair of sloth bears came woofing near the machan. Confused, they also stopped there for a while. This gave the General enough time to shoot one, while the other was able to get away. The shot sloth bear also dropped on the ground close to where the tiger lay.

Two loud whistles from the General was the pre-decided signal to the beaters that the tiger was dead, and that they could now come up to the machan. A little later the beaters and the elephants reached the spot, fetching the mahouts who had been placed on trees as 'stops'. In his enthusiasm of seeing the dead tiger and the bear, Ishtiaq started to climb down from the elephant but was strictly reprimanded by Latafat Ali mahout not to do so yet.

Latafat was Ishtiaq's uncle under whom he had been trained during his early years. The experienced mahout told Ishtiaq that a sloth bear can be very dangerous if injured, and before approaching one, it should be clearly ascertained that it was indeed dead, and not just looking dead.

Latafat walked his elephant slowly up to the the sloth bear, circling it slowly to look for any sign of life. Sure enough, the sloth bear suddenly came to life and made a mad rush towards the line of beaters gathered on the ground. Fortunately, the General was ready for such an eventuality, and his next shot dropped the sloth bear dead.

When the Tiger had the Last Laugh

And for me, this last *shikar* tale narrated by Ishtiaq is the *piece de resistance.* Too many times we see hapless tigers being shot by men with high powered rifles from the safety of their perch in the machan or elephant back. But this is one story in which the tiger was the winner, while the *shikari* lost his precious sphincter as well as his vanity. So please pardon me the wicked glee with which I write this.

In 1962, Ishtiaq was on duty in the Lansdowne Working Plan where SS Srivastava was the Working Plan Officer, and BP Srivastava was the Conservator, Working Plans. As mentioned earlier, BP Srivastava was a very keen *shikari*, and usually had a string of guests who were facilitated by him to go on a tiger hunt. And most of the time, the services of Ishtiaq were requisitioned by him on such occasions.

One day, there was a letter from the Conservator to the WPO that one of his special guests, an army Colonel, was coming to their area for a tiger hunt, and that Ishtiaq should ensure that the Colonel had a successful tiger shoot in the Mithawali shooting block. Ishtiaq promptly reached Mithawali FRH at the appointed date and presented himself before the Colonel who had arrived there with his daughter.

Ishtiaq suggested to the Colonel that next morning, he would take him around on the elephant to recce the forests to identify the most likely place for the tiger shoot. Studying the lay of the land, it was finally decided that shooting a tiger from a machan over a live bait would bring better results rather than scouring the forests on an elephant to find a tiger.

Two live baits were procured and on the next day, one of them was tied at a likely spot where there were chances that a tiger would appear. The spot they chose was a confluence of two small streams, and the numerous pugmarks there indicated that it was a regular beat of the tiger. A good strong tree was also present there, from which the machan would give a clear and expansive view of the bait and the surrounding areas.

So Ishtiaq and his *characut* tied a cot on the tree and placed a

mattress on it to provide a comfortable seat. The live bait was then tied near the water flowing in the streams. After Ishtiaq and the Colonel had comfortably settled in the machan, the *characut* was ordered to take the elephant away, only to return when the men on the machan gave him the signal that all was clear and that it was safe for him to approach. The Colonel kept the rifle in his possession and handed his spare .12 bore shotgun to Ishtiaq, telling him that he was free to use it in case the need arose.

Now both men sat quietly on their vigil to await the arrival of the tiger. Presently, the moaning call of a tiger was heard. The men were now in a heightened state of nerves, expecting the tiger to come into view any time now. However, the tiger did not appear, although he kept up the moaning call. Suddenly another tiger called, and it became clear to them that there were not one, but two tigers in the vicinity.

Both tigers kept up their calls for some time, while the men on the machan peered around trying to spot them. It was only after a wait of about half an hour that a huge male tiger appeared on the scene. As he caught sight of the *katra* (bait) he froze in his tracks. He then calmly sat down on the ground in front of the *katra*, looking at it.

Ishtiaq thought it was a great time to take the shot, but the Colonel wasn't moving. Ishtiaq says that he nudged him lightly, motioning him to shoot. But the Colonel brushed him away and putting his finger to his lip, whispered '*shush*'. So Ishtiaq stayed quiet, waiting for the Colonel to lift his rifle and take the shot. But nothing of that sort happened. Suddenly the tigress also appeared and joined its mate at staring at the *katra*, which was now in a frenzied state of fear at the sight of the two tigers so close by. Again, Ishtiaq nudged the Colonel and pointed with his nose at the large male. Once again, the Colonel responded with a stern look and a hissed '*shush*'.

So Ishtiaq sat back quietly to await the Colonel's next move. Suddenly, the male tiger gathered his hind legs in a crouch and rushed at the *katra*, seizing it by the throat and brought it down to the ground. He kept holding on till its life slowly ebbed away. All this while, the tigress kept sitting quietly, watching the proceedings. An impatient Ishtiaq looked towards the Colonel, exhorting him with his eyes to shoot, but the Colonel evaded his eyes and remained sitting.

The *katra* was dead by now and the tiger gave one mighty jerk and broke the rope. He started dragging it away into thick cover, with the tigress following close behind. Ishtiaq's last desperate nudge again drew no response, as both tigers disappeared from sight.

Ishtiaq says that it was then that he felt the foul smell emanating from the Colonel. At first, Ishtiaq discretely held his hand over his nostrils, then took out his handkerchief and tied it like a bandana across his face. It was now evident that the Colonel had not just wet his pants, but done much more. He turned to the stony-eyed Colonel and asked, "*Sahib, haathi bula loon?*" (Sir, should I call for the elephant?) The Colonel gave him a pathetic nod of acquiescence. He also took out twenty rupees and gave them to Ishtiaq without saying anything. Ishtiaq nodded understandingly and pocketed the money.

He then blew on his whistle, which was the signal to the *characut* to come and pick them up from the machan. Since no shot had been fired, and there was no chance of an injured tiger, the *characut* came on merrily. As soon as the elephant came near the machan, Ishtiaq ordered the *characut*, "*Haathi pay say gadda hata day.*" (Remove the mattress from the elephant's back.). The *characut* failed to comprehend this command and did not move. Ishtiaq again repeated the command, but this time too, the *characut* did not understand what he was supposed to do.

So Ishtiaq turned around to the Colonel and whispered, "*Sahib, yeh sab ko bataa dega.*" (Sir, he is sure to tell everyone.) The Colonel took out another twenty rupees and gave them to Ishtiaq, who passed them on to the *characut*, which was promptly pocketed. Ishtiaq knew that now the time had come to spill the beans. He asked the *characut*, "*Tujhay pata hai sahib ne tujhe inaam kyun diya hai?* (Do you know why you have been rewarded by the sahib?) It was obvious that the *characut* had no clue, and replied in the negative. So Ishtiaq was now blunt and to the point. "*Abay, Karnal sahib ki latrine nikal gayi hai.*

Kisi say kahiyo mati. Ab gadda hata day," (The Colonel sahib has had a faecal discharge. Don't you dare tell this to anyone. Now remove the mattress).

This time the *characut* complied with swift alacrity and the mattress was hurriedly removed to save it from being soiled. The embarrassed would-be *shikari* and his two bemused companions now started on their return journey to camp, leaving behind the smelly signs of the Colonel's trepidation on the machan. Arriving at a stream on the way, which was a good distance away from the streams where the tiger pair must have been feeding on their own free reward from the Colonel, a halt was called and the Colonel dismounted to wash up. He sent Ishtiaq to the FRH to get him a clean pair of trousers and underwear.

Al the FRH, Ishtiaq called out to his daughter. She came out and asked where her Daddy was. Ishtiaq told her, "*Sahib keechar may gir gaye thay. Unkay kapray kharab ho gaye hain. Unka ek patloon aur kachcha de do, Bibi*" (The sahib had fallen in the mud and his clothes have become soiled. Please give me a pair of trousers and underwear for him").

A very contrite Colonel decided to break camp the very next morning. He was probably keen to exit the scene of his mortification as quickly as possible. Before going, however, he called Ishtiaq and asked him, "*Tumharay paas kuchh paisay hain?*" (Do you have some money?) A confused Ishtiaq told him that he had only two rupees in his pocket. The Colonel asked him to hand him the two rupees, saying by way of explanation, "I had bought two *katras*, of which one had been eaten by the tiger. I give you the remaining one for these two rupees".

And then the Colonel left, leaving Ishtiaq the reluctant owner of a buffalo calf worth two rupees. He did however write a great complimentary comment for Ishtiaq in the FRH register.

Maybe someday, if I happen to pass Mithawali FRH, it would be great to read the Colonel's comment if that invaluable register is not already lost to the sands of time.

Later, when Conservator BP Srivastava came that way, he ruefully asked Ishtiaq why he had failed to make the Colonel's tiger shoot a success. But Ishtiaq told him tongue-in-cheek, *"Sahib mai nahi bata sakta hoon, mujhay bees rupaye diye hain"* (Sir I can't tell you that. He has given me twenty rupees). Ishtiaq was the Conservator's favourite and was therefore allowed the liberty of speaking freely. The Conservator laughingly told him to let out the secret. Ishtiaq then recounted the entire sequence of events, along with the faecal ending.

"Theek hai, aisay aadmi ke saath tumhara koi kaam nahi hai" (All right, a man like this doesn't deserve your skills). "But did he give you any reward?", the Conservator asked. "*Na koi Sir. Chhup rehne ke bees rupaye ke alawa kuchh nahi. Balki ulta mujhse do rupaye le gaye*" (Nary a reward Sir, apart from the hush-money of twenty rupees. On the contrary he took away two rupees from me).

We had a hearty laugh right through the time Ishtiaq was narrating it. At the end of the story. I asked Ishtiaq whether he remembered the name of the Colonel. He sounded regretful, saying that it had slipped from his memory. But I was happy. I thought it was just as well. At least I would not be bound to ever give a name to this 'unknown soldier'.

CHAPTER 9

All Ishtiaq's Elephants

An elephant is an extension of the mahout who rides it, and vice-versa. The mahout - elephant relationship cannot work seamlessly unless both strike a strong bond with each other. And that inherent bond between man and animal is based on mutual respect and love. The long years Ishtiaq spent as a mahout in the forest department, brought him in contact with many elephants that were allotted to him. Just like humans, he said, each had some characteristic all its own, and the analysis of these differences was the key for him to be able to control those different elephants.

Ishtiaq's association with elephants had started way back in 1949, after his vagrant life in Rampur had prompted his mother to send him off to Ramnagar, to be under the care and tutelage of his maternal uncle Latafat Ali. Ishtiaq admitted that he was quite chastened at having had to leave his home, so took it upon himself to mend his ways. He said that he worked really hard with Latafat Ali, and tried to learn all that was taught to him. Only three years of intense tutoring and training under Latafat Ali brought out in him the qualities of elephant care and management, and a life-long career as a mahout.

This brought our discussion to the inevitable question about the various elephants that had come under his care and management during all the years that he served as a mahout in the Forest Department. As our conversation veered on this subject, Ishtiaq started recalling from memory most of the elephants he drove.

The first elephant that he worked with was called **Ram Kali**. His association with her started in 1952 when he was freshly appointed as a *characut* under his uncle Himayat Ali. Soon after Ishtiaq joined him, Himayat Ali was posted to Lakhimpur Forest Division for mahout duties in the Working Plan, under Conservator GM Hopkins.

Himayat Ali proceeded to his new assignment along with his *characut* Ishtiaq. It was here that Himayat Ali and Ishtiaq came in contact with the elephant Ram Kali for the first time. She had been previously assigned duties in the Silviculture Department in the *terai* forests, where she had been shot at by some cultivator while she was out grazing, and had ravaged his sugarcane field. As a result, she had a bullet wound on her right foreleg, which had developed into a deep abscess, rendering her incapable of performing her duties

Because of her seemingly incurable wound, and the intense pain that she would probably be suffering, the Conservator ordered that she be shot to put her out of misery. But Himayat Ali intervened in the execution of this order and begged the Conservator for one chance of trying to treat her. The Conservator thought hard, but ultimately rescinded his decision and allowed Himayat Ali to go ahead and try out his remedy to treat Ram Kali.

The first step in the treatment required surgical intervention. But there were no surgical tools, and the only things available were a pair of large scissors and an *ustura* (barbers' shaving blade). Himayat ordered Ishtiaq to go and hone the *ustura* sharp. They then lay the elephant down and tied all four legs together by an iron chain. Himayat commenced the surgery by incising the skin around the wound and told Ishtiaq to take out the pus and infected gore that lay inside.

Ishtiaq recalls that the wound was so deep that most of his hand would go in to scrape out all the infected tissue. It was clear that the bullet had hit low, but had deflected after impacting the bone, and had lodged much higher than the entry point. Whenever the wound was operated and cleaned earlier, it used to provide temporary relief, but the medicine could never reach the actual wound where the bullet was lodged. After some time, pus from the top used to percolate down and cause the entire wound to be infected again. Hence the elephant had to be repeatedly kept off duty.

This time, Himayat gave an incision over the actual wound. And when Ishtiaq cleaned out the tissue mass from there, the flesh was blackened and burnt. Himayat then gave him the *ustura* and told him to remove the skin from around that area. It was a difficult job to take out the one and a half-inch thick hide of the elephant, which was lying hobbled on the ground, trumpeting with pain, but kept restrained by Himayat's *ankush*.

Eventually, when the whole patch of the skin was removed, Himayat filled up the wound with the previously prepared medicine. He still kept the elephant lying down on the ground to prevent the medicine from draining out if she was allowed to stand upright.

When Conservator Hopkins came to know about this operation, he came personally, accompanied by the Range Officer, to see how things were proceeding. Hopkins enquired Himayat Ali, "Mahout, what are the chances? Will she be alright?" Himayat answered, "Yes Sir, she'll be all right soon." But the Range Officer was sceptical, "Himayat, you have made her incapacitated for 3-4 years, so big is the wound you have made". But Himayat said, "*Sahib*, I assure you she would be fine in six months". Almost true to his words she came back on duty in the seventh month.

After completing the Working Plan assignments, Ishtiaq was posted in 1957 to the Bahraich Forest Division, where he was ordered to take charge of a new female elephant named **Sita Kali**. She was very young and had been purchased from an elephant dealer by the Forest Department. She was still so small in size that Ishtiaq could clean her back while standing next to her.

It was around 1959 during this posting, that the DFO SM Sibtain ordered Ishtiaq's promotion as a mahout. On the day of his promotion, the DFO told Ishtiaq, "You are the first person whom I am promoting as a mahout. There should be nothing that undermines my confidence in you". A grateful Ishtiaq replied, "Sir, I shall never do anything that spoils your name." After Ishtiaq's transfer back from Bahraich to Ramnagar in 1960, he gave up charge of Sita Kali, and his short interaction with her ended.

He then spent about two years in his posting at Ramnagar doing miscellaneous assignments. In 1962, the mahout assigned on **Champa** elephant reached his retirement age. This paved the way for Ishtiaq being allotted Champa under his charge. She stayed continuously with him till 1969, the year he had to take a hiatus from his forest department job. He was away from the department for nine continuous years, although he kept in touch with his officers who kept calling on him regularly for errands and short assignments.

Thereafter in 1978, Ishtiaq was called back to service in the forest department by CB Singh who was Director, Corbett Park. He had procured two new elephants for the park, named Gomti and Rapti. The latter died quite soon after being procured, but Gomti lived to serve for a long time. Incidentally, she was the same elephant which later figured in Subedar Ali's mauling by the tiger Sheroo.

When Ishtiaq re-joined the forest department, he was allotted charge of **Gomti**. Talking of Gomti's fickleness, Ishtiaq says that initially, she used to panic and run away even when she encountered chitals in the forest. She was absolutely untrained when she came to Ishtiaq. Her walk was very uneven and mahouts and *characuts* found it difficult to ride her bareback. But gradually she settled down to being a good safari elephant and served with Ishtiaq for a few years before she was allocated to another mahout Subedar Ali. This decision apparently caused some resentment within Ishtiaq, who thought it reeked of undue favouritism, but he was ultimately brought around to accepting the reasons for this dispossession.

After Gomti, Ishtiaq was given an elephant called **Malan Kali** whose mahout Basheer had retired from service. She served under Ishtiaq as a safari elephant in Dhikala but was unfortunately bitten by a cobra on her tongue. She had the habit of sleeping with her mouth open and tongue lolling out. There was an old septic tank that had been dug for a proposed toilet, but since the toilet was never made, the tank ultimately turned into a garbage pit. A large-sized cobra staked its claim on the pit and started living in it. It had been spotted many times before but had never hurt anyone.

Although the actual bite to Malan Kali was not witnessed by anyone, it was Ishtiaq's surmise that it was this very cobra that had made its way into the *feelkhana* in the quest of rodents that were usually found feeding on titbits strewn around from the elephants' rations.

One morning Ishtiaq got up at 5 AM, later than his usual time of 4.30 AM, to prepare his elephant for the morning safari He hurriedly picked up the *roti* (flour pancake) prepared the previous night for his elephant, and headed straight to the *feelkhana* to feed it to Malan Kali. Usually, she took the *roti* straight into her mouth, but on that day, she took it in her trunk. As Ishtiaq turned to go, he saw that Malan Kali had put the *roti* on the ground. He was perplexed and returned to the elephant. Giving her a once over, he saw that there was a thin watery discharge from her trunk. He had been taught that in case of a snake bite, the elephant would show symptoms of a bloated stomach, and a watery discharge from the trunk.

He examined her stomach and felt that it was distended. This was worrisome and needed immediate remedy. He recalled that his *ustad* (mentor-teacher) had always taught him that if an elephant falls sick, the mahout should always discuss it with other mahouts and knowledgeable persons, to first confirm the ailment and only then proceed to medication.

The people Ishtiaq called for consultation were Eidu mahout and Shaukat mahout. Eidu had previously been Ishtiaq's *characut* and had been trained under him to become a mahout. Eidu refrained from forwarding any opinion on the matter and demurred by saying that Ishtiaq was the better judge of such things. However, Shaukat opined that the elephant had swallowed mud and its ailment was temporary and of no great consequence. Ishtiaq silently differed with that opinion but Shaukat was insistent, advising Ishtiaq to pad up the elephant and take it out on duty.

Before doing so, Ishtiaq went to the Ranger and informed him of his apprehension that Malan Kali had been bitten by a snake. The Ranger and Ishtiaq together then went to Director CB Singh's camp-residence to give him this information. He was having a bath, but told Ishtiaq to go ahead and start the necessary medication, and that he would follow soon. When Ishtiaq reached Malan Kali to haul up the *gadda* on her back, he felt her body trembling. He quickly jumped off the elephant, thinking that if she fell, he might be crushed under her body. As soon as he jumped off, she made a mad run-around and then fell heavily on the ground.

Seeing her fall, Basheer mahout's son, who happened to be a *characut*, thought that since the elephant had a bloated stomach, possibly its dung had hardened and blocked the rectal passage. He took matters into his own hands and shoved his hand in and started kneading the rectum to draw out the dung. Ishtiaq says that as soon as she fell, her eyes had lost the light and lustre, and he knew for sure that she was dead. He again rushed towards the Ranger's residence and broke the news that Malan Kali was dead.

The tragic death of Malan Kali due to snake bite.

As soon as word spread amongst the mahouts and *characuts*, Ishtiaq's wife and children were also awoken by the commotion. Realising what had happened, they started weeping and wailing at the death of their elephant. Eidu mahout's wife consoled the kids by saying that they had no reason to cry since it was just a government elephant and that they would soon get another one in its place. But Ishtiaq's wife retorted by saying that the elephant was not just an animal but like a family member and the very means that provided sustenance to her family. Ishtiaq recalled that for three days no food was cooked in his house, as they all remained in shock and mourning.

After Malan Kali's death, Ishtiaq was put on miscellaneous duties in Dhikala for some time, and then came in possession of his last elephant, **Rambha.** This happened in 1984 when CB Singh was the Chief Conservator, Wildlife and Ashok Singh was Director, Corbett Park. Rambha was then stationed for duties at Khinanauli FRH. One day, while disciplining Rambha for her disobedience to him, her mahout had inadvertently injured her with a spear, somewhere in the region of her toenail. Her injury aggravated and her foot swelled so much that she could not walk.

CB Singh happened to visit Khinanauli soon after. Rambha had always been his favourite elephant, and it was common knowledge that he loved her immensely. He always made it a point to feed the *roti* to her with his own hands. She also used to respond by quickly coming over to him whenever he called her by name.

When he called her on this particular occasion, she did not appear. After repeated calls, he walked to the *feelkhana*, and seeing her there, he admonished her for not responding to his calls. "*Badmash, pehchan nahin rahi hai?*" he asked, failing to notice her inflamed foot. When Rambha saw him, she twanked her trunk on the ground, squealing pitiably in pain. It was then that CB Singh saw her injury, and cried out in sorrow and in anger. "Who has done this?" he thundered. He immediately ordered Ashok Singh to suspend her errant mahout, and put some other mahout in charge of Rambha. It was decided by officials to allot Rambha to Ishtiaq since he was without an elephant at that time.

On the question of why she was speared by her mahout in the first place, the story goes that it happened in a rare fit of anger. The mahout had taken her down to the Ramganga river for her daily bath, and she had refused to sit in the water as ordered by the mahout. His angry stab with the spear inadvertently injured her in the wrong spot. The toe-nail area of an elephant's foot carries a sensitive network of nerves and veins, and the injury there caused the aggravation in her foot.

Ishtiaq arrived at Khinanauli to take charge of Rambha. He requested the Director to allow him to nurse her at Dhikala. His request was acceded to by the Director on the condition that she be brought to Dhikala only when she was able to walk properly.

Ishtiaq got to work on her foot and was able to undo the inflammation by the third day. He then triumphantly walked her to Dhikala. He went to the Director and requested him to come and see Rambha. He casually told Ishtiaq that he planned to go to Khinanauli FRH on the morrow, and would see her then. So Ishtiaq smilingly told him that she was present in Dhikala. A pleasantly surprised and happy Ashok Singh came straight to see her at the *feelkhana*. He praised Ishtiaq for the quick and effective treatment and assured him that Rambha would now be permanently under his charge.

And thus, Rambha came to Ishtiaq as his last, but longest-serving companion in Corbett Park. And when they came together, their team became something of a legend for the people who got a chance to ride with them.

However, this wonderful team had to go through a sort of betrothal by fire, which happened in the very early stages of their association. Ishtiaq recalled that before Rambha was allotted to him, she had a mind of her own. She used to be strong-headed enough to overlook the mahout's commands, caring none the less for her misbehaviour. If the mahout wanted to be strict with her, she wouldn't think twice before shaking her body violently and making the mahout and riders fall off her back. She once dislodged Park Director CB Singh from her back at Gaithia Rao. Another person she shook off her back was a park official named Gaur.

Ishtiaq astride his favourite elephant Rambha

When she came to Ishtiaq, she initially tended to be headstrong and displayed her independent behaviour. He opined that elephants are quite like human kids, and have the same qualities of disobedience and stubbornness as some kids have. It is therefore incumbent upon the mahout to deal with them firmly so that they can learn that they have to show obedience and good behaviour when dealing with the mahout. He wistfully stated that he gave Rambha so much love and kindness that she never misbehaved with him during all the years she stayed under his charge.

There was only one exception however, when Ishtiaq had to deal with Rambha with an iron hand. This happened during the early years when the process of building the mahout-elephant relationship was on between Ishtiaq and Rambha. At that time Ishtiaq had to work without his *characut* who had proceeded on long leave. For almost one and half months, Ishtiaq handled Rambha without a *characut*. It was a tough and gruelling work to go twice a day on elephant safaris, and in the intervening time, get green fodder from the forest, as well as take the elephant down to the river for her daily bath and cleaning rituals. Although Ishtiaq had his young son Irfan to lend a helping hand, most of the daily chores had to be performed by Ishtiaq himself.

One day, when Ishtiaq returned from cutting fodder in the afternoon, he sat down to have a quick lunch. He asked his daughter to fill two buckets of water and keep them ready so that post-lunch he could clean up a dirty Rambha and then get her padded up in time for the afternoon safari. He went to the *feelkhana*, unshackled her and brought her over for a wash. As soon as Rambha saw the buckets she ran away, leaving Ishtiaq surprised and angry. He knew that there was just a little time left for him to get her ready and report at the elephant station in time for the safari. Ishtiaq ran after her, caught her lead rope and ordered her to sit down so he could start saddling her. But she was in an adamant and disobedient mood.

Those were the early days of their association and she still was as headstrong as she had been with her earlier mahout. She kicked out at Ishtiaq with her hind leg. He evaded that, but her swinging tail caught him on the temple. That hurt him and made him angrier at her insolence. He called out to his daughter to fetch the cane kept in his shack. By the time the cane arrived, he was in a fit of rage and he started lashing out at Rambha. He recalls that it must have been about an hour that the lashing went on.

His shouted expletives while he beat her, and Rambha's bellows created a commotion that attracted several tourists and staff, who gathered around Buddhi Kala's canteen to witness the disciplining of Rambha. After some time, a few tourists couldn't bear the sight of the elephant being beaten, and ran over to the reception to complain to the in-charge Karketi, asking him to make the mahout stop the beating. Karketi knew the ways of the mahouts and placated them by saying that if the mahout was in the process of disciplining his elephant, he wasn't likely to stop till it was done.

The fracas ended when Rambha finally submitted by falling on her knees and resting her head on the ground. An exhausted and uncontrollably enraged Ishtiaq hissed out a warning to her, to never repeat such a misdemeanour with him again. The intelligent elephant probably understood Ishtiaq's stern warning, because from then on, she fully submitted to Ishtiaq, and never repeated any disobedience. But on that day as a punishment, Ishtiaq made Rambha walk the forest for about ten kilometres, instead of the usual three or four kilometres that are covered by an elephant during the safari.

Some days later, but only in playfulness, she refused to come out of the Ramganga river when it was time for her to get back to camp for the evening safari. Ishtiaq had sent his sons Irfan and Rizwan to go and get her back from the river, but try as they may, Rambha would not listen to their commands. RN Pandey, the Deputy Director was in his residence overlooking the river, and he saw that when the boys went into the water to fetch Rambha, she would not come out and even showed some aggression towards them.

Worried about their safety, he went over to Ishtiaq's shack to direct him to go down and control the situation. Ishtiaq quickly made his way down to the river where Rambha was happily gambolling in the water. Reaching the water's edge, he called out a short warning to the elephant.

On hearing him, Rambha quickly responded with the soft *'pussu'*, indicating that she was coming out, and like a good elephant, she came on Ishtiaq's heel back to camp.

RN Pandey had seen the goings-on and later complimented Ishtiaq on his absolute verbal control over the animal, even at the time when she was being disobedient and aggressive with his sons. However, those were early days, when their relationship was building up before it eventually developed into the strongest of bonds that Ishtiaq had with any other elephant that he controlled before Rambha.

Ishtiaq's son Irfan on Rambha, with RO Narendra Singh Chaudhary, Characut Muneer and Forest Guard Mehra

When Rambha died, she had been with Ishtiaq for almost 14 years. Her death marked the end of Ishtiaq's career as a mahout in the forest department. He spent the remaining years of his service in performing miscellaneous duties in Dhikala, till he attained the age of superannuation.

CHAPTER 10

On the Trail of the Man-eaters

Corbett Park has had a few cases of tigers becoming man-eaters, and this subject was sure to draw a great response from Ishtiaq. He has been on many a trail for the man-eater, and we hoped to make him talk about some of his experiences. Since he was speaking from memory, there was an element of randomness in his narrative, and that's the way it goes.

The Kothi Rao Man-eater

Ishtiaq recalls the case of the tigress which had attacked and killed a retired military man in the forests near Kothi Rao, a small village that lay somewhere between Jhirna and Dhela. It was a small village with a few houses, and the military man who was killed belonged to this village. Surrounding the village were dense forests and a *sot* (spring) that supplied water to a fairly deep pool.

One day, a party of people numbering about twelve was going across that pool to collect the strong vines that are used for making ropes. As the party crossed the pool, they were suddenly attacked by a tigress. She sprang at the military man with such viciousness that her lashing forepaw struck a rock with great force after crushing the man's skull. The blow was so powerful that when it hit the rock, three of its claws left a deep impression on it. The man died on the spot, but before the tigress could drag him away into the forest his companions, including his wife, regained their wits and started shouting in unison. This scared the tigress, who then left her victim and ran off into the forest.

The men then retrieved the body of the dead man and carried it to the main road where the residents of Kothi Rao gathered and sat on a protest against the Forest Department. They demanded that the tigress be immediately dealt with since it was now a potent threat to their lives.

The Park Director Ashok Singh ordered the Corbett Park Research Officer AN Singh and Deputy Director RN Pandey to immediately reach the spot and prepare a report of events so that a decision about the future course of action could be taken. Although both officers had the services of Shafi mahout who had been requisitioned from nearby Bijrani FRH, they felt that his elephant was not adequately trained for tracking the man-eater.

So they sent instructions to Dhikala that Ishtiaq and his elephant Rambha make a start immediately and report to them at Kothi Rao. Ishtiaq was able to reach Kalagarh by evening that day and since there were no living quarters in Kothi Rao for him and his elephant, he halted at Kalagarh to spend the night there and to rest his elephant after its exhausting journey.

The next morning, he promptly reached Kothi Rao and reported to his officers. Before they started, there was a great sense of expectancy among the villagers gathered there that the tigress would be quickly eliminated by the team of officers present there. Before they started on their mission from Kothi Rao, the widow of the dead man again reiterated that the tigress which had killed her husband was sure to have three of her claws blunted by the force with which she had raked the rock with her paw.

AN Singh and RN Pandey were mounted on Ishtiaq's elephant while Shafi and his elephant brought up the rear. When they reached the spot where the man was killed, they came upon the tigress. She was sitting on the ground where she had killed the man and was now licking the ground where splashes of blood from her victim were still lying congealed.

It was a great position to take a shot at the tigress and put her out of action then and there, but not having clear orders from the park Director to shoot the man-eater, both AN Singh and RN Pandey dithered in taking the shot that would put a quick end to her short and dubious career. Ishtiaq put in his forceful submission to the officers that in case the tigress was not shot immediately, he would not dare to spend the night at Kothi Rao with a man-eater prowling close, since there were no safe living quarters for him and his elephant.

The short debate between them ended when RN Pandey assured AN Singh that he would later secure the Director's permission for shooting the tigress.

AN Singh was ready all the while, and now he took the shot. While they had been dithering, the tigress had started moving away, and when the shot was taken, only a small portion of her body was visible while she was almost fully hidden behind some boulders. If the shot was not taken immediately, she would melt into the forest and not be seen again.

As the bullet found its mark on the little target that was visible of her body, she sprang up and tried running up the adjoining incline, but then fell back rolling down the slope. She crawled roaring and spitting towards Shafi's elephant Roopkali, which panicked at the sight and ran off wildly in the opposite direction. But Rambha stood steadfast, thus allowing AN Singh to take steady aim and drop her dead with a spine shot.

When her death throes had subsided completely, Ishtiaq got down from his elephant to check her paws. Sure enough, he saw that its three claws were blunted. This was proof that they had shot the right animal and everyone was glad at this quick operation. It was decided to take the tigress to Kothi Rao and display it to the widow of the victim so that her anger and sorrow could be assuaged.

The tigress was hauled up onto Rambha's back and taken to the hamlet. Once again, the widow took a keen personal interest in seeing the forepaws herself, after which she declared that she was satisfied that the real culprit had been punished.

Within no time the village *Patwari* and other residents also gathered around the dead tigress and broke into a celebration of sorts, rejoicing that the scourge had been eliminated. Celebrations over, the tigress was tied onto the bonnet of AN Singh's jeep and driven to Ramnagar, the Corbett Park headquarters.

And yes, the formal permission for shooting the tigress was secured by the officials, although *ex post facto.*

The Bijrani Man-eater

One morning, four women belonging to a village called Ringora, near Bijrani went out into the forest to cut grass. As they sat down a little distance from each other, talking and cutting grass, they came in close range of a tiger which was lying hidden nearby in the tall grass Suddenly the tiger rushed out, ran a short distance, and caught hold of one of the women. However, as usually happens with the brave women of the hills, the other three showed immense courage by standing their ground, shouting and brandishing their scythes in the air to scare the tiger away and save their companion if possible.

But the tiger roared back in defiance and refused to relinquish his kill, holding on to the woman just a short distance away. The three women could see that their companion was dead by now, but were still determined to recover her body from the tiger. So they set fire to the patch of grass. As the burning grass spread towards the tiger, he left his kill and ran off, leaving the body of the woman. The three plucky women now dragged the body away from the burning grass, and then raised the alarm.

As news spread about this incident, the local residents got together and angrily laid siege to the Park Director's residence in Ramnagar. Director AS Negi assured the residents of quick action in killing the aberrant tiger. His staff swung into action, a machan was quickly set up over the kill-site and the Director, along with AN Singh, climbed onto the machan to await the return of the tiger.

It is not clear to me how they managed to do so, but they prevailed upon the local residents and the dead woman's family to allow her body to remain at the spot where she had been killed, so that they would have a better chance to shoot the tiger when he returned to reclaim his kill. The tiger arrived, and as he came in view of the machan, the Director fired at him. The bullet hit him in the neck region, but he did not fall and escaped into the nearby forest.

The officials now had no other option but to follow up on the wounded tiger. By now it was growing dark, so they had to postpone the follow-up operation till the next morning. Since following-up on an injured tiger required a staunch elephant and a skilful mahout, the Director sent a wireless message to

Dhikala, ordering Ishtiaq to come immediately to Ramnagar with his elephant Rambha.

It was around 8 PM that Warden Suresh Pant came to Ishtiaq's house to inform him that the Director had ordered him to start for Bijrani immediately. Pant informed him that he had orders to remain with Ishtiaq till the time he commenced on his journey. He was to then send information to the Director confirming that Ishtiaq had actually started from Dhikala. Sensing the urgency of the directives, Ishtiaq quickly got his elephant ready, but since the journey was to be undertaken all through the night, he requested Suresh Pant for an armed guard to accompany him. Pant assigned an armed guard named Mehra to go with Ishtiaq.

They travelled all night on the Dhikala-Dhangadhi road, reaching Sultan FRH just as dawn was breaking on the horizon. Since Rambha was now quite tired because of the night-long walk of about 30 km, Ishtiaq called the journey to a halt to rest his elephant and his companions.

As soon as he stopped at the Sultan FRH, the staff posted there came to him with a wireless set to enquire how soon he would be leaving for Ramnagar. They said this had to be done in compliance with the Director's orders that Ishtiaq's movement be monitored and reported to him at all times. Ishtiaq told his *characut* to unshackle Rambha's howdah, give her fodder and water, and allow her to rest while they also had tea and breakfast at the FRH. A couple of hours later they were again ready to resume their journey.

On reaching Dhangadhi gate, Ishtiaq was once again accosted by the official there, immediately sending the message of his arrival. Ishtiaq jocularly remarked to them that he had by now started feeling very honoured, the way he was being monitored and reported at every point.

I asked Ishtiaq whether there was any shorter forest route that he could have taken to reach Bijrani directly, and why he had to take the longer road route. He answered that his destination was not Bijrani but a place called Semal Chaur which was much easier accessed from Amdanda gate. Moreover, navigating the elephant through the forest in the night darkness was not a viable option at all.

When they reached Ringora, about two km inside the Amdanda gate, he saw that his son-in-law was also present there. On asking him why he was there, the son-in-law smilingly replied that he was there only because the wireless messages ringing across the forest network were announcing that 'Papa' was arriving there. One would surely concede that it must have been a proud moment for Ishtiaq at the importance being accorded to him, and it was amply conveyed by his smiling face when he was narrating this story.

As soon as Ishtiaq reached Semal Chaur, he found that the Director had also arrived there with ample packets of food in his vehicle. The good officer knew that his men coming from Dhikala would be starved after their long journey. The Director made them all have a hearty meal and told them to rest for a while, after which they would all go after the man-eater's pursuit at around 4 PM.

At the appointed time, the Director and AN Singh mounted Ishtiaq's elephant to go after the injured tiger. But first, they went to look at the spot where the shot had been taken at the tiger last evening, and determine the angle of the shot from the machan. This would help them to assess the place where the bullet had hit the tiger, and analyse the blood trail to determine the extent of its injury. Both officers were referring to the man-eater as being a male tiger, but when Ishtiaq picked up its pugmarks from the spot, he was quite sure that it was a female. He cockily entered into an argument with the officers about the tiger's gender, trying to convince them that they were mistaken about the man-eater being a male.

As I listened to his story, it seemed incredible to me that such senior and experienced officers could have been so naïve to insist that it was a male when the pugmarks before them indicated that it was a tigress. I interrupted Ishtiaq and asked how that could be possible. He smilingly conceded that of course, the officers were right, and this was one of those times when he found himself on a sticky wicket about his jungle knowledge. Actually, the Director had noticed the tiger's genitals at the time he took the shot, although he did admit that the pugmarks were presenting a confusing picture.

The examination of the blood trail left by the tiger indicated to them that its injury was not serious enough to kill it immediately, although it was likely to die eventually. But there was very little hope that if they went looking for the tiger immediately, they would find it either dead or near death. It was clear that they had an injured and potentially dangerous animal to deal with.

Since searching for such an animal on an elephant in a vast forest area was quite unfeasible, they decided to end the search operation, and rather use a live bait instead. Since it was getting dark, the bait was tied at a likely spot and left overnight in the hope that it would be killed by the tiger.

Next morning the bait was found alive, and there were no signs of the tiger having appeared there. Once again the bait was left tied there, albeit with a longer rope and a vessel of water for it to drink from. By evening it was still untouched. The officers now returned to Ramnagar, putting Ishtiaq in charge of monitoring the situation, and sending them word when required.

On the third morning too, there was no sign of the tiger, so Ishtiaq had the bait removed from the spot it had been tied and brought it back to Ringora. He was perplexed at the tiger's sudden disappearance and even started having doubts about his own assessment of the extent of the bullet injury. He was now thinking that contrary to his assessment that the injury was not fatal, maybe the tiger had after all died somewhere in the forest. He looked for vultures in the sky to reinforce this surmise, but there were none to be seen.

Sometime in the afternoon, the canteen owner from Bijrani FRH came running with the information that a tiger was seen sitting near the FRH, and that Rashid *characut* (later mahout) had sent him to call Ishtiaq. When he reached Bijrani FRH, Rashid informed him that the tiger had been spotted near the nearby waterhole. Rashid and the canteen owner also mounted the elephant with Ishtiaq, to go with him and take a closer look at the tiger. Before going however, Ishtiaq warned Gopal, the forester posted at the FRH that the tiger could be the injured man-eater, so he should ensure that all the staff members present at the FRH remained indoors and kept their doors closed

The tiger had moved away from the place where it had been sitting. They followed its pugmarks on the sandy soil, which then took them to a patch of forest where they saw the tiger lying down on the ground on its side. When the tiger saw the elephant approaching, he slowly got up and started moving away without giving them a chance to see if there was any injury on its body. When the elephant reached the spot where the tiger had been lying, Rambha instinctively kicked at the spot, spraying it with dry mud. I reasoned that this action was probably her effort to obliterate the strong tiger smell that must have assailed her senses.

The tiger quickly moved away into the forest and was lost to sight. Since there was nothing that the unarmed men could do by following it any further, they returned to the spot where the tiger had been lying. Ishtiaq said he wanted to observe if the tiger had left any sign that might indicate that it was injured. He knew the injury was now about four days old so there were hardly any chances of finding blood, but if the injury was suppurating by now, it was sure to leave some pus or fluid.

Ishtiaq got down from the elephant and sat on his haunches peering at the spot. A few minutes later he saw two green maggot-flies alighting at the spot, and he was now able to see the little discharge which had attracted the flies. This was enough confirmation that the man-eater was near at hand. Quickly remounting the elephant, they headed back to the FRH and asked Gopal to go immediately to Ramnagar and inform the Director and AN Singh. Although the Director did not come due to his official preoccupation, AN Singh was there within no time. He instructed the men to have their lunch and then be ready to go in pursuit of the tiger.

Soon AN Singh was mounted with Ishtiaq on Rambha, and they all started the search for the tiger. This time the party was accompanied by two other elephants, one manned by Kallu mahout and the other by Sardar mahout. It took them a long time to search for the tiger, but without a sight of him. Presently they came upon a patch of dried lantana bushes. AN Singh directed Ishtiaq to search in that patch, and sure enough, when the elephant entered the patch, the tiger was sighted lying hidden under it.

As the elephant bore down upon his hiding place, the tiger quickly got up and started a loping run towards heavy cover. When Ishtiaq quickly got Rambha to cut off his escape route, the tiger stopped in his tracks, giving AN Singh a clear shot. But they were still not able to see the side on which the tiger had been injured, so the shot was held back in a bid to confirm that this was in fact the injured tiger.

Suddenly, the tiger put his neck sideways on the ground and started sliding for a few feet. It was then that they all realized that the wound in its neck was festering and full of maggots. Irritated by the twitching insects in his neck wound, the tiger was desperately trying to dislodge them by rubbing his neck on the ground. Unable to reach the wound with his tongue to lick it clean, the poor tiger had been suffering the aggravation and infestation for four days.

Getting up from the ground, the tiger was in the process of climbing a small incline, when he presented a good target to AN Singh. This time the bullet struck the tiger at the right spot, and though he did make a last rush across the incline, it was evident that he was not going too far. They decided to wait for some time and then they moved the elephants to the other side of the incline, where they found the tiger stone-dead.

Ishtiaq got down from his elephant to confirm why the pugmarks of the tiger had confused him into thinking that it was a tigress. Indeed, the hind pugmarks of the tiger were found to have elongated toes and could have passed off as being those of a tigress.

Mission over, the man-eater was brought back to Ramnagar after the customary display at Ringora village, so that the inhabitants in general, and the dead woman's family in particular, could assure themselves that the man-eater striking was dead.

L – R: Sardar mahout, Kallu mahout, Bachan Ram driver, AN Singh, Ishtiaq mahout, and Shareef mahout with the Bijrani man-eater.

As for the confusion created by this tiger's peculiar pugmarks, it is worth mentioning that a close look at the hind feet in the photograph of the dead tiger may help the discerning reader to reach a logical conclusion of his own.

The Bhooki Tigress of Dhikala

Ishtiaq recalled the incident of a very *bhooki* (hungry) tigress that ventured right into Dhikala camp and attacked two staff members, Sher Bahadur *characut* and Shafi mahout on the same night. He said that it happened on the '*chand raat*' of 1988.

Chand raat is usually referred to as the night on which the new moon is sighted, marking the Muslim festival of Eid-u-Fitr the following day. By deduction, I put down the date of this incident to 17th May 1988. A new-moon night is a dark night. The darkness was further compounded by the fact that there was an electric fault in Dhikala that night. Since there was no threat perception of a tiger attack within Dhikala camp, the staff members did not think twice before going off to sleep in their shacks with open doors. The open doors would at least let in a draught of breeze into the rooms to help them beat the heat of that stifling night.

Sometime past midnight, a tigress slunk quietly into the camp and made her way to the area where the mahouts and *characuts* had their shacks. Her first victim was Sher Bahadur, a Nepali *characut* who was sleeping with his family inside his shack. As he lay sleeping, he was caught by the tigress and dragged out of the room. His shout of alarm woke the neighbourhood, and in no time a yelling crowd gathered. In the ensuing commotion, the tigress left him and slipped into the darkness. The injured man was attended to with first aid, and then driven off to Ramnagar hospital for further treatment.

As the excitement and commotion died down in Dhikala, the staff members returned to their shacks, this time closing their doors for fear of the tigress returning. Although she had melted into the darkness, they knew that she could still be lurking quietly to make another attempt.

Unfortunately, this is exactly what happened. Shafi mahout was in the process of shutting his door when he was attacked by the tigress who had sneaked back into camp. She caught Shafi and tried to drag him away but somehow, she could not do so. At that time, the Park Director Ashok Singh and Brijendra Singh happened to be present in Dhikala and had been on the lookout for the animal after the first attack. As the tigress came into view, they quickly took the decision of shooting her there and then.

The tigress turned out to be an injured and starving animal. Her injuries were maggot-ridden and it seemed that she had not fed for days. Demented by hunger and pain, she had made a desperate bid to come into Dhikala and attack the men. It was no wonder that in her pathetic physical condition, she was unable to kill either of her intended victims. Fortunately, both men recovered fully from the tigress' attack within a few days.

While ending the story, Ishtiaq smiled ruefully and said, '*Us taygress ko mar diya jaana uske liye rehmat ho gayi.*' (Killing that tigress was like an act of mercy for her) That wise comment stood quite to reason. Since her physical condition had deteriorated beyond any treatment or natural recovery, she would have died of her injuries anyway. It was therefore good thinking by the vigilant park officials that her misery was put to an end that night.

The Man-eater of Pantnagar

This man-eater story goes back to much older times, when eliminating man-eating tigers did not involve the process of tranquilizing or trapping, as devised in later years. Back then, it was then just a matter of shooting them down, and the only thing required was the availability of an officer willing to do so.

Narrating this story, Ishtiaq mentioned that the man-eater was shot by Stevenson of the Pantnagar University. Backtracking on this little piece of information, one finds that Dr Kenneth Anthony Parker Stevenson was the first Vice-Chancellor of the GB Pant Agriculture University located in Pantnagar, about two km from Lalkuan. Since his tenure as VC was from December 1958 to January 1964, it can be safely assumed that this was the duration between which Ishtiaq's story is dated. Further, since Ishtiaq got reposted to Ramnagar in 1960, and was allotted the hunting elephant Champa in 1962, the date of this hunt can further be narrowed down to between 1962 and 1964. Be that as it may, let's move on to the story.

This man-eater became active in the areas around the Pantnagar Agricultural University, and within a short period, killed three persons. Stevenson was a hunter himself, and when he expressed his resolve to shoot this man-eater, he received the necessary permission from the forest department. To help Stevenson in this mission, the Conservator even assigned his two elephants to be used for tracking and shooting the tiger. Ishtiaq was one of the two mahouts who brought their elephants to Pantnagar to report their arrival to Stevenson.

After a couple of days, a live bait was killed by the tiger, and the mahouts were able to locate the area where he was lying up in the morning after a hearty meal. But the mahouts informed Stevenson that only two elephants would be inadequate for a beat in the area where the tiger was lying up. So, another two elephants were quickly provided by the Working Plan Officer at Haldwani, and now the four elephants were ready to start the beat.

A machan had been set up, and Stevenson took his position to await the tiger when it was driven his way. The beat started and the tiger promptly came into Stevenson's view. He took the shot, but the bullet hit the tiger in the pelvic region. Though injured, it was able to get away. Giving the injured tiger adequate time to settle down, the follow-up operation was launched about an hour after the shot had been taken. Only three elephants were used now, while the fourth was placed as reserve some distance away.

As the three elephants started following the blood trail left by the tiger, it suddenly rushed out from a bush in which it was hiding and attacked the elephant which was driven by Ishtiaq's younger brother Akhlaq. He was a *characut* in Haldwani forest division and was manning the elephant in the absence of his mahout who was on leave.

The tiger's sudden attack made Akhlaq's elephant squeal in terror and pain. Seeing his plight, the mahout of the third elephant, on which Stevenson was mounted, brought his elephant running to the injured one's rescue. As he reached near, the oncoming elephant kicked out at the tiger. The enraged and wounded tiger now turned his attention to this elephant. He took a flying leap and latched onto its face, digging his sharp claws deep around the eyes.

 In utter panic, the elephant shook its head vigorously in a bid to dislodge its tormenter. However, this panic-stricken move unbalanced the elephant, making it fall forward on its forehead. Whether it actually fell forward or was using the standard aggressive move of elephants to crush their victim under their head, is something that is unclear. There was a real danger of Stevenson falling off the elephant while it jerked and swerved in its struggle with the tiger. What saved the day for Stevenson was that he had been sitting firmly in the howdah, and although he was not able to take a shot at the tiger in all this ensuing commotion, he did well to hold on to his seat and thus escaped from falling off from the elephant, onto the enraged tiger below.

As the tiger felt the weight of the elephant's forehead bearing down on his body, he released his hold on the elephant's face and ran away into the forest. With both elephants belonging to the Haldwani forest division now injured, and the enraged tiger still around somewhere, Ishtiaq too lost his nerve and goaded his elephant to run away in the direction the other two elephants had taken. He ruefully admitted that it was only after the elephant had run scared for about one km that he managed to make it halt.

When the elephants regrouped after the panic caused by the tiger's attack had subsided, Stevenson took stock of the situation. He decided that since Ishtiaq's elephant was the only one uninjured, he would now go after the tiger with Ishtiaq. The mahouts of the two wounded elephants were directed to go back to Pantnagar to have their injuries attended to, and to take along the third elephant which had been stationed some distance away and had not been a part of the follow-up operation.

Now it was Ishtiaq's elephant on which Stevenson resumed the search for the tiger. Handing over his .12 bore shotgun to Ishtiaq, and keeping the heavy rifle ready in his own hands, Stevenson told Ishtiaq to fire away as soon as the tiger was sighted. As they started traversing through the forest to look for the tiger, they were both quite nervous. This could be gauged from their jumpy reaction when they both fired into a bush where they thought they could see the twitching ears of a tiger. It was only when some startled little birds flew out from the bush that they realized their folly.

Barely had they recovered from their panic-stricken reaction and reloaded their weapons, that out came the tiger roaring and charging towards their elephant. Probably he was still enraged enough to cross swords with the humans who had injured him. But this time Ishtiaq held his elephant steadfastly, and before the charging tiger could inflict damage again, Stevenson's shot ripped through his body, dropping him dead in his tracks.

In later years, there were a few more man-eaters in Corbett Park who became famous for their misdeeds. The ones most of us remember are Sheroo and Dhitoo. Their stories have been narrated at length by Ishtiaq, and consequently, I shall dwell upon these tigers individually, and in some detail.

CHAPTER 11

Sheroo, and the Killing of Kukku

The conversation with Ishtiaq inevitably turned to the tigers that had turned to man-eating in Corbett Park. And there could have been no better tiger to embark on this subject than the one called Sheroo. He was the same tiger who figured in the killing of a *characut* called Kukku and later in the mauling of another *characut* named Subedar Ali.

According to Ishtiaq, it was around 1980 or 1981 that this huge tiger started becoming infamous. His great size and his bold ways quickly made him a much-sighted tiger in the Corbett Park. It should be remembered here that those were times when tigers behaved as tigers should normally do - by being elusive and rarely sighted in the wild. They were not like tigers which are encountered in tiger reserves nowadays, fully visible and seemingly undeterred by the convoy of Gypsy vehicles surrounding them and antics of the hordes of chattering tourists and irritating shutter-bugs in the vehicles.

So it was natural that a wild tiger like Sheroo, who could be so frequently sighted by tourists and officials alike, would become a well-known tiger of Corbett Park. Very soon, this tiger became a favourite of the Park Director CB Singh, who tracked, baited and photographed him regularly. In fact, it was CB Singh who christened this tiger as 'Sheroo'.

Sheroo used to inhabit the area ranging from Bichubhoji to Chuipani. In Ishtiaq's opinion, the fearlessness and aggression in the tiger's behaviour were indicative of the fact that Sheroo had lost all fear of humans. Such tigers usually refuse to back down or slink away in the face of a man-animal conflict. The local mahouts were of the view that Sheroo had probably been in conflict situations before, and it was quite likely that Sheroo might one day go beyond fearlessness to downright aggression with humans.

It was not long before Sheroo's aggressive propensity was officially confirmed when he killed Kukku, a *characut* posted at Dhikala under Kallu mahout. Kukku was the son of a forest guide named Howard, who was a tourist guide based at Dhikala. This incident happened in March 1982

As was his routine every day, Kukku had taken his elephant Chetna into the forest to cut its fodder and bring it back to camp. After they had crossed the Ramganga river and the grasslands, they reached the Chuipani Sot area. There were enough trees here to provide good tender branches and leaves for fodder. Dismounting from the elephant, Kukku put the hobble-chain on the elephant's legs and climbed up on a large tree to lop off the branches with his axe.

Unknown to him, Sheroo was also in the area and had zeroed in on him. He kept himself hidden from view and impatiently kept waiting for his intended victim to get down from the tree. His impatience was clear from the fact that he lay down at three different places near the tree while he waited for his intended quarry's descent from the tree.

When Kukku had finished cutting the fodder, he climbed down the tree. *Characuts* normally gather the lopped branches into a large, neat bundle and then haul it up on their elephant's back. But when Kukku came down, he found that his elephant had drifted some distance away while feeding. So he proceeded to walk up to Chetna to bring her back to where the lopped branches were lying. But before he could reach his elephant, he was attacked by Sheroo on a rocky incline which Kukku had started to climb to reach the place where the elephant was standing.

Sheroo attacked him from behind, making him fall forward. Then he grabbed his neck and quickly dragged him off into the forest. The commotion of the attack and the growls of the tiger while attacking Kukku, must have scared the elephant away and she was now left unattended without her *characut*. Admittedly, there was no human witness who could corroborate the sequence of events but later, when the rescue teams went to recover Kukku's body, they saw all the signs and tried to reconstruct the events as they may have happened.

For the entire day, Kukku and his elephant were not missed at Dhikala camp. It was around dusk that Kallu mahout mentioned to other mahouts and staff members that neither his elephant nor his *characut* had returned from the forest. Ishtiaq remembers that he and others berated Kallu on this great lapse. They were all of the view that if the elephant and *characut* had not made it back to camp by 2 PM, he should have raised the alarm.

So they all hurriedly went to the Park reception office and informed the official on duty. As soon as word reached the higher officials, a search party was sent to find Kukku and his elephant. Since Kukku had gone out alone, there was no one who could identify which specific area he had gone to. So all that the search party could do was to drive their elephants on the forest road cutting across the Dhikala grassland, stopping now and then to yell out Kukku's name in the hope that if he was in some distress he would call back.

But there was no response from the missing man and after a futile effort, the team returned without a trace of either Kukku or the elephant. It was now quite late in the evening, they all headed back to camp. It was decided that they would continue the search on the morrow.

Next morning, when the elephants went out with tourists for the jungle safari, Kukku's elephant Chetna was found grazing in the Bichubhoji area. She was spotted by Sharafat mahout, who rounded her up and brought her back to Dhikala camp. On examination of the elephant, it was found that Kukku's *dhoti*, which he must have taken off before climbing the tree, had been tied on the strapping rope. But it was torn and tattered.

This indicated that the *dhoti* must have been torn by tree branches when the elephant had suddenly been scared and had made a mad dash into the forest. This raised doubts that some serious mishap had befallen Kukku, and spurred the mahouts and *characuts* into action. Soon, a search party on elephants once again headed towards the Bichubhoji area where Kukku's elephant Chetna had been found.

When they reached the spot, they found an incline where footmarks of the elephant indicated that it had run down in a hurry. They surmised that it was here that the elephant had dashed down in panic. Backtracking on the tell-tale signs they reached the other side of the incline when they found splashes of blood, Kukku's cap and his axe lying on the ground.

They left the axe and cap at the spot and returned immediately to report to the Park Director that the *characut* had been killed by a tiger. Once the matter was reported, the officials also joined in to return to the spot and investigate the incident in detail.

The search party comprised of Deputy Ranger Indraj Singh, and mahouts Ishtiaq, Hameed, Kallu and other staff members. When they reached the incline where the incident had taken place, Ishtiaq suggested to Indraj Singh that recovery of the dead body would be more effective if it was done by walking on the ground and following the tracks closely, rather than from elephant- back.

Volunteering for this job, Ishtiaq, Indraj Singh, Hameed mahout and a couple of staff members got off their elephants. They started following the tracks, which were clear at some places and indistinct at others.

At this point, I asked Ishtiaq whether they all knew that it was Sheroo they were after. He replied that they had no confirmation that it was Sheroo since it could have been just any tiger.

Although they lost the tracks on the rocky surface, they knew fully well that the tiger had taken this very route carrying his unfortunate victim. Ishtiaq says that he almost doubled up to look closely at a rounded object that could have been mistaken for a rocky pebble, but looking closely, he identified it as a piece of bone with the little blood on it. When he turned it over with a stick it was identified as the ball from the pelvic girdle which had probably been left after the tiger had chewed on the leg.

This indicated that the body had been eaten somewhere nearby. This was a relatively soft spot and here they found the clear print of a single pugmark. The pugmark indicated it to be a male tiger. Near that spot was a grassy area where the tiger had made a full meal of the man. What remained were some pieces of the bones of the thigh and arms, which were discarded after being chewed up. Apart from that, the tiger had eaten up almost the entire body.

They returned to Dhikala where Park Director CB Singh had by then informed the Police under the standard legal procedure in such cases. That very day, Brijendra Singh also arrived at Corbett. and he had a machan erected near the remains of Kukku to await the arrival of the killer tiger. It was not long before the tiger returned to the kill, and there remained no doubt that the erring tiger was indeed Sheroo.

Kukku's father Howard was also informed of the sad occurrence and then taken by the Director and Police to the spot so that he could recover whatever remained of the unfortunate Kukku, to perform his last rites.

But Sheroo was still not condemned as a man-eater due to the forest department policy that no tiger can be killed or captured until it can be ascertained that he has deliberately killed two or more humans. This was reason enough for the Park officials to let Sheroo continue to live a free life in Corbett Park, and possibly it was a god-sent opportunity for the officials too since it allowed them to carry on their observation, viewing and filming of their favourite tiger.

Two years passed, and the death of Kukku was gradually forgotten. The wide berth that the mahouts and *characuts* used to give to the Chuipani Sot area out of fear of Sheroo, gradually diminished too. Slowly but steadily, they once again started making forays into the area either during elephant safaris or to cut fodder for their elephants. This was just the recipe for another impending disaster, but nobody was willing to consider the possibility of Sheroo striking again.

CHAPTER 12

Sheroo and the Mauling of Subedar Ali

Two years after Kukku's killing, Sheroo attacked another man, a Corbett Park *characut* named Subedar Ali. At the time of the attack, Subedar Ali was a *characut*, but since his mahout was away on a long leave of absence, he was also holding the charge of mahout.

The attack took place on 15th February 1984 when Subedar went out on his elephant Gomti, along with his companion, another *characut* named Qutub, who was mounted on his elephant Mauli. Both elephants went to the very spot at Chuipani where Kukku had been killed almost two years earlier.

Recounting the events of that fateful day, Qutub said that when he came up to the first suitable tree, he decided he would cut the elephant fodder from this one. So, he swung up from his elephant's back on to the tree and started lopping the leaves.

Likewise, Subedar Ali also went about 200 yards ahead to a spot that adjoined a hillock under which there was a suitable tree that stood quite tall on the roadside, but whose overhanging branches were not very high on top of the hillock. Subedar halted Gomti on the road near the tree and hobbled her a short distance away.

He then proceeded to climb the tree to cut fodder. It seems that while all this human activity and was going on, Sheroo had been either in the vicinity, or the sounds of the axe on wood attracted him. He arrived at the scene and lay down hidden in the undergrowth on the top of the hillock. This was the side where the branches of the tree were not very high. Subedar Ali was among these very branches lopping the leaves and letting them fall below to the ground. He must have all along been under the gaze of Sheroo.

After enough leaves had been cut, Subedar started his descent from the tree, using his axe to disentangle the branches that had got stuck on the tree. As he came within striking distance, Shero leapt at the man, catching hold of him. In this process, however, both man and tiger fell not on the hillock, but deep on the roadside.

Both tiger and human crashed heavily on the ground, the tiger landing on his back, with the man on top of his underbelly. Possibly hurt in the fall the tiger lashed out instinctively at the weight on his belly, and in the process raking the head of the man with his claws so that the scalp came off from the back of the head to hang inverted onto the face.

Subedar later recounted graphic details of the attack and his lucky survival as he remembered it, but at the time of the attack, his shouting out to Qutub for help and possibly the sounds of the tiger alerted his companion who quickly brought his elephant Mauli running to the spot, lashing her with his bamboo stick, urging her to run fast. Probably the pain of the lashing or the close presence of the tiger made Mauli trumpet in anger or fear, which added to the noise and confusion. Sheroo then left the man and sat about 8 yards away on the opposite side of the road.

As soon as Qutub reached the spot, he placed his elephant between the tiger and the fallen man, yelling out instructions to Subedar to try and release his elephant's hobble chain and climb up on its back. Qutub was aware that if he himself took the chance of climbing down from his elephant to rescue

Subedar, he would be putting himself in grave danger, since the angry tiger was still sitting nearby.

Subedar Ali, after recovery from the tiger attack.

Somehow Subedar managed to crawl to his elephant and unshackle her, whereupon she lifted him on her back. The injured, half-conscious Subedar now held on to his elephant for dear life, as the two elephants fast-paced towards the camp. The tiger followed them for about one kilometre and then disappeared into the jungle.

When they reached Dhikala, Director CB Singh promptly arranged for Subedar to be driven to the hospital in Kashipur about 58 km away. Subedar was treated there for a few days until Brijendra Singh intervened, and had him admitted to the prestigious AIIMS (All India Institute of Medical Sciences) Delhi, where he remained under treatment for a long time.

Recounting this incident, Ishtiaq expressed a little scepticism at Subedar's survival story in which he famously punched the tiger in the face, shoved his fingers into its eyes, bit its nose, and put his hand inside the tiger's mouth and clutched its tongue. In Ishtiaq's opinion, a strong tiger like Sheroo would not have dithered in getting a stranglehold on his victim's neck unless he was himself quite injured or dazed by his long fall when he launched his attack on Subedar.

Ishtiaq quotes Qutub as saying that when he reached the attack site on his elephant, yelling and charging, he saw that the tiger was sitting away from the injured Subedar, and so he had the opportunity to quickly position his elephant Mauli between the injured man and the tiger.

Whatever may have been the reason for the tiger not pressing home the attack on its victim, the delay gave Subedar that vital window of opportunity which allowed him to be hauled up on the back of his elephant Gomti.

Ishtiaq's scepticism may be ascribed to either professional rivalry or jealousy. That incident had given Subedar Ali huge global publicity, and he became a celebrated and much sought-after mahout at Corbett Park, with many stories written, and films made about his escapade. If this caused a bit of jealousy and heartburn in Subedar Ali's colleagues, including Ishtiaq, it may be quite understandable.

However, it is also a valid contention by Ishtiaq that the tiger might not have been able to press home its attack due to the injury it suffered when it fell down the ridge with Subedar on top of him.

Be that as it may, the attack on Subedar Ali paved the way for Sheroo's capture, because it was now not possible for the officials to shield him and let him roam free in Corbett Park any longer.

CHAPTER 13

Sheroo's Capture

Since the attack on Subedar Ali was Sheroo's second misdemeanour, it was perforce decided by the authorities that he should now be removed from Corbett Park since he had become a potential threat to humans. Orders to this effect were issued by the Chief Wildlife Warden at Lucknow. It was now a foregone conclusion that Sheroo would soon be captured or shot dead by the Corbett Park officials.

But first, standard operative procedures required that the identity of the tiger be ascertained beyond any doubt. The officials had a record of Sheroo's pugmarks right since the time he had killed Kukku, and when they compared them with those of the tiger which attacked Subedar Ali, they matched perfectly.

So the next step was to place a cage with a trapdoor in the vicinity of the place where Subedar Ali was attacked. A live bait was tied near the cage to attract Sheroo to the area. But Sheroo remained elusive and refused to kill the bait. The officials scoured the forest to look for him, but he seemed to have vanished from the area.

Then one morning there were glad tidings that the bait had been killed by a tiger, and its pugmarks indicated that it was Sheroo. The officials now had the bait tied to an elephant and dragged into the cage, after which the trap door was set up. Although there were signs that Sheroo was lurking somewhere close by, he did not enter the cage that evening.

It was only when they returned to the spot early the next morning, that they found Sheroo trapped in the cage. The constant chatter of the men when they saw their quarry in the cage, and the frightened trumpeting of the elephants at the sight and smell of their dreaded adversary, caused Sheroo to let out earth-shaking roars.

Sheroo's Capture: Ishtiaq sitting with a black cap near the cage,

As caged carnivores usually do, he repeatedly banged his head against the bars of the constricted cage, hurting himself considerably. It was a sorry sight to see the once majestic tiger with his bloodied nose and facial injuries inflicted by himself in his futile attempts to break free.

I asked Ishtiaq how many people were present when Sheroo was trapped. Ishtiaq informed that there was Director CB Singh, AN Singh, Brijendra Singh, Ishtiaq himself, Eidu mahout, and a few more staff members. They had all gone on their elephants to see if the tiger had been trapped.

It was only after the men and elephants had moved away from the spot, and a covering sheet had been draped over the cage, that Sheroo eventually calmed down. A truck was then requisitioned from Ramnagar. When it arrived, the cage was hauled onto it, and Sheroo started his long road journey to Kanpur Zoo and a miserable life of captivity. Sheroo was captured on 28th February 1984, exactly 13 days after he attacked Subedar Ali.

In response to my query about how long Sheroo ruled as the dominant male in the Dhikala area, Ishtiaq said he reigned supreme for about 8 to 9 years. Although Ishtiaq had no idea about Sheroo's lineage, he did confirm that his genes must surely have been dispersed in the Corbett Park gene pool, since he mated with several tigresses during the period when he was the dominant male in Corbett Park.

Mohammed Ahsan, IFS mentions in his book *The Wild Tales* that during the period Sheroo was incarcerated in Kanpur Zoo, he also mated with a captive white tigress named Seema, and she gave birth to three cubs.

CHAPTER 14

Dhitoo, and the Tragedy of David Hunt

One of the most well-known tigers to have roamed the Corbett Park was called *Dhitoo* (stubborn). This was the name given to him by the Park Director CB Singh, who was posted in Corbett Park when this remarkably bold tiger was making his presence felt in the tiger reserve.

According to Ishtiaq, this tiger was quite immense in proportions and had characteristics all his own. Over a period of time, he had developed the unnerving habit of approaching quite close to the tourists' vehicles. He was also known to come dangerously close to the safari elephants too, and in the process became a frequently sighted and much-photographed tiger. Dhitoo was known to frequent an area close to Gaithiarao *kund* or pool, on the farther side of the Ramganga river that flows to the north of Dhikala and Khinanauli forest rest houses.

Whenever he was encountered on the forest roads, it was his nature never to side-step or give way. But if the vehicle was parked to the side and he was given the right of way, he would pass by quite close to it. However, if he felt that the passage given to him was not adequate or to his liking, he used to lie right across the road in front of the vehicle and remonstrate forcefully all the while. But during all these close encounters that he had with tourist vehicles or safari elephants, there was hardly any incident that resulted in any threat or injury to human life.

Ishtiaq recalls one incident that gave him a clear inkling of the impending danger to human life that Dhitoo could likely pose in the future. It happened in the early 1980s when an elderly British tourist had come to Corbett, very eager to see and photograph a tiger. The Range Officer took note of his intense enthusiasm and called up Ishtiaq. "Look, I have promised this gentleman that you will show him a tiger today. So you go along with him in his vehicle and ensure that he does see one", he told Ishtiaq.

Although Ishtiaq pointedly told the Range Officer that the promise he had made to the tourist bordered on extreme optimism, and also tended to place a huge responsibility on him, he agreed that he would nevertheless try his best to help the tourist fulfil his wish. So, he boarded the vehicle along with the tourist and his driver.

They quartered the forests for the entire afternoon without any sign or sight of the tiger. As the day drew to a close, and it seemed to the dejected party that it was time to return to camp, Ishtiaq told the driver that it might be a good idea if they utilized the remaining half-hour to look up the Gaithiarao area in the hope of meeting up with a tiger there.

So off they went to Gaithiarao, where there was a large pool of water. As they neared the pool from the western side, they saw a fully eaten chital kill, with only the skin and some bones remaining. The signs and smells indicated the proximity of the tiger. Looking around, they saw a dark shape lying on the farther edge of the pool. With mounting excitement, Ishtiaq peered at the shape in a bid to identify it.

Almost simultaneously the tourist, who was watching through his powerful binoculars, let out a great gasp. "A very huge tiger!" he hissed. Now they could make out that it was indeed a tiger lolling half in and half out of the water. The tourist was in a state of high excitement and begged Ishtiaq to do anything that would make the tiger come out of the water and into the last of the remaining light so that he could film this tiger.

There seemed no other way but to get off the vehicle and try to disturb the tiger from his resting place. Ishtiaq was half certain that the tiger could be Dhitoo, so he reluctantly, and a bit fearfully, got off after telling the driver to keep the door open to allow him to quickly enter the vehicle, in case the tiger was Dhitoo and decided to give chase.

As he neared the water's edge, he felt that the tiger was watching him intently from where he lay on the other side. But summoning courage, he put his hand in the water and splashed it. As soon as he did so, the tiger let out an angry roar and dashed across the pool towards him. Handicapped as the tiger was with having to wade through the water, Ishtiaq was just able to reach the vehicle and clamber into safety.

It was now quite evident that the tiger was indeed Dhitoo, for he came straight to the vehicle where the three men remained motionless, although the tourist did keep his camera rolling. Dhitoo however did not seem to be in too much of a rage for he only gave small twitches of his lips in silent snarls. He came up to the vehicle and stopped to sniff at the front tyre for a few seconds. He then walked away slowly on the forest road leading to the Ramganga river, while the humans followed in the vehicle, keeping it at a reasonably safe distance so as not to alarm him again.

After crossing the two rafter bridges across the river, Dhitoo finally stepped into thick forests when it was almost dark, leaving an excited and highly satisfied party to return to Dhikala camp.

Later that evening, sitting with his friends and other staff members, Ishtiaq discussed the entire incident, and also opined that the way Dhitoo had charged up to him when he was on foot, it seemed that the charge was not a mock one, but would have been driven home if Ishtiaq had not been able to make it into the vehicle in time. But it was sometime before this foreboding became a reality.

In February 1985, a team of birdwatchers led by a British ornithologist named David Hunt, came to visit Corbett Park. The end of winters is an ideal time for bird-watching, when Dhikala is virtually stormed by a multitude of local and migratory species of birds. Many groups of birdwatchers descend on Corbett from all parts of the world, and it is during this time that the majority of tourists fanning out into the forest on vehicles or riding elephants relegate the tiger to the second spot, the first one being taken up by the birds.

During such excursions, it is often a common problem for a lone animal lover to find himself on a riding elephant in the company of three other chirpy bird-watchers who exult loudly whenever a bird is spotted. Ishtiaq admits that the mahouts too sense the priorities of the riders sitting on the elephant. So when the riders are identified as bird-watchers or *chirimaars*, as the Corbett staff calls them, the mahout invariably lets the elephant tread on meandering forest paths which promise more sighting of birds rather than the elusive tiger.

David Hunt's group of birdwatchers was a well-organized one, consisting of twenty two members. Arriving at Dhikala in the afternoon, they walked in a group around the camp, confining their bird-watching activities only to the grassland in that area.

However, the next morning's program was a meticulously planned one. It was scheduled to start at dawn, with an elephant ride from Dhikala which would take them northwards across the Ramganga river and grasslands, and on to the start of the forest road which leads up to Kanda - the highest point of Corbett tiger reserve, made famous by the man-eating tiger shot there by Jim Corbett.

Once they arrived at this point, a pre-requisitioned minibus would meet them and take them on their further journey into the thick forests to the north, where an excellent day of bird watching awaited the group. Four elephants had been reserved for the party for the early morning ride from Dhikala, while Harak Singh Aswal, a Corbett Park staff member who was a recognized expert on birds, was assigned the duty of guiding the party on its day-long trip.

David Bassil Hunt (1934-1985)

His tragic death on 23rd February 1985 in Corbett Park left his friends reeling in stunned disbelief, overwhelmed by the sudden irreplaceable loss.

In recounting the sad details of David's tragic story, the author wishes to convey his deep condolences to them.

Ishtiaq recalled that he was one of the mahouts when the party left early from Dhikala on four elephants. As they crossed the river and the expansive grassland beyond, they were exhilarated by the bounties which the forest had to offer them. They encountered herds of chital and elephant, but it was the multitude of birds that they focused on. It took the elephants about two hours to complete the stretch of the grassland, and arrive at the forest road on the other side, where the vehicle awaited them.

The change of transportation was quickly made, and now the birdwatchers took up the next stage of their journey in the vehicle, while the mahouts guided the four elephants on the return journey to Dhikala camp. Since Ishtiaq was one of the mahouts who took that return journey, he was not present when tragedy struck the birdwatchers. But what happened later became the focal talking point in Corbett tiger reserve, and possibly does not lack anything in detail as far as recounting of the actual incident goes.

Having gone a little towards the farther side of Gaithiarao, the birdwatchers came upon a large owl. They quickly got off the bus, and in a flurry of activity brought out their binoculars and cameras to zoom in on the bird. This went on for a while, until the owl took off from the bough it sat on, and glided to another tree a little further away.

Most of the birdwatchers returned to the bus, but David Hunt and two others followed the owl to the next tree. When it flew away once more, to sit on a third tree, the other two also trudged back to the bus. But David Hunt seemed to be so fixated that he walked on alone into the dense forest towards where the owl perched now.

When his last two companions reached the bus, they were all ready to leave. But when they said that David Hunt was still out there, the other group members started getting restive, impatient to continue their journey. Harak Singh was feeling concerned and angry at the foolhardiness of the man. Was he not aware that this was not just a walk in a park, but actual tiger territory? Didn't he realize that to walk alone in such an area was fraught with danger?

After waiting for a few minutes, Harak Singh was finally convinced that it was time to go and round him up. Taking his gun, and the last two companions of David Hunt to indicate the spot where they had last left the man, they went in the general direction where the owl had been first sighted. Following on from there, they reached the spot where the companions pointed to the *dhang* – or ridge, where they had last seen David Hunt climbing while following the owl. The grim silence of the area conveyed to them that something was amiss. The nervous companions now insisted that they would like to go back to the bus.

After they left, Harak Singh was now left all alone, and he carefully moved forward to the place where David had walked. As Harak Singh climbed up the ridge and reached the top, he heard the low growl of a tiger and simultaneously saw David Hunt lying dead, with the tiger sitting a few feet away from the body.

Unsure of what to do next, Harak Singh quietly backed off and ran to the bus, where he broke the news of David's killing to the group. There was panic and confusion amongst the members, and no one seemed certain about what to do under the circumstances. It was mutually decided that since the tiger was in the vicinity, there was nothing that could be done for David Hunt. It was evident that there was no other option but to return to Dhikala and report the matter to the higher officials.

On reaching camp, the matter was reported to the Park Director. He promptly ordered that immediate arrangements be made to retrieve the body. This was a matter involving the death of a British national and was hence going to be a serious diplomatic issue. Six elephants were readied for the retrieval job, Ishtiaq being one of the mahouts. The rescue party also consisted of the Director, the Deputy Director, Range Officer, Harak Singh, and other staff members. They promptly started for the spot where the attack had been made.

Before leaving for the rescue mission, the Director had issued instructions to his staff to secure written testimonials from all the group members specifying that the death of David Hunt was caused due to personal negligence and that the forest department was not at fault. This was willingly and truthfully declared by the group members.

When the rescue party reached the spot, they found that the tiger had dragged the victim's body further away from the point where he had been killed. By now it had also eaten a portion from the right thigh. It took them quite a long time to make the tiger give up its kill. Anyone who knows cat behaviour will understand that retrieving even a house-cat's kill is a difficult job.

It was with considerable effort that the six elephants were able to push the tiger away. He eventually gave way, and sat down a little further away, remonstrating loudly. While four elephants were made to stand guard to prevent the tiger from breaking back, two elephants moved to the spot where the body lay. Two staff members quickly got down to the ground and hauled it onto an elephant. Now the rescue party started on its return journey to Dhikala camp.

It may be questioned here that the rescue party was fully armed and they had the aberrant tiger fully in sight with all the evidence of his misdemeanour, so why did they not decide to shoot him there and then? The answer lay in the department's procedure which specifies that a man-eater can only be shot after an executive order is issued by the state Chief Wildlife Warden.

And so, investigations were started to prove beyond doubt that it was Dhitoo who was responsible for the death of David Hunt. Moreover, this was deemed to be Dhitoo's first human kill, which did not prove beyond doubt that he was a confirmed man-eater, and so the executive order was not issued. Be that as may, Dhitoo earned an immediate reprieve from being eliminated that day.

Back at the camp, the other tourists who were part of that bird-watching party reacted to the news of David Hunt's death with a mixed feeling of horror and sadness at the loss of their group leader, who was a jovial personality and had become friends to many in the group.

I asked Ishtiaq to describe the state of the body when it was retrieved from the tiger. He said that indications were that the tiger had initially used his front paw to swipe at the face and bring David down. He then proceeded to bite the back of the neck, killing him. The body had been covered with mud and dried leaves in the process of being dragged away from the attack site. When recovered, the tiger had eaten only about 2 – 3 kilos from the right thigh, while the rest of the body was intact.

Since it was evening by the time the rescue party returned to the camp, the body was left in the charge of the mahouts, including Ishtiaq, who were instructed to guard it for the night. It was laid on a *charpoy* under the tin shed behind the reception area, while the staff sat around a bonfire, guarding it all through that cold February night.

Earlier in the day, a forest department staff member had been sent to New Delhi to contact officials of the British High Commission and seek instructions about procedures to be undertaken for David. The British High Commission made arrangements to carry the body to New Delhi, about 250 km away. David Hunt was cremated in New Delhi on 25th February, and the ashes were flown back to Britain, to be scattered by his family in the waters off Tresco, in the Isles of Scilly in Cornwall.

In ending the unfortunate saga of David Hunt, my deepest sympathies go out once again to his family and friends.

However, it may be recalled that Ishtiaq had mentioned much earlier that Dhitoo's aggressive behaviour with humans, and his bold approach towards them, was indicative of the fact that he might have been in conflict situations with humans before, especially with the nomadic *Gujjar* tribe. These are cattle-herders who intrude into the Corbett Park area from the northern boundary and let their cattle graze on the lush foliage late into the evenings, and sometimes all through the night.

I am also a witness to their late-night forays into the Park. I was sitting in Buddhi Kala's canteen in Dhikala for supper one evening when I saw lights moving near the watchtower located on the north, across the Ramganga river. Initially, I thought it was forest staff stationed there for night duty. But Ishtiaq, who was sitting with me, informed that it was *Gujjars* who may have stayed on to spend the night to let their buffalo herds graze in the forest through the night.

To me, it seemed incredulous and foolhardy for the *Gujjars* to expose themselves and their cattle to attacks in these tiger-infested forests at night. But Ishtiaq informed me that *Gujjars* are a brave lot and have no fear of tigers when in the company of their herds and that their buffalo are fiercely combative against tiger attacks, which they ward off by forming a close circle of horns, effectively blocking the tiger

If one has to believe Ishtiaq's contention that Dhitoo had attacked and eaten men from this tribe before, it is supported by the fact that *Gujjars* are a close-knit society, totally dependent on the forests for their cattle's needs. A few isolated cases of tiger attacks on them may have gone purposely unreported for fear of imposition of stricter measures by

Police and forest department against their unfettered entry into the forests.

Investigations were started by the forest department to ascertain the actual identity of the tiger which had killed David Hunt. The pugmarks of the tiger were taken from around the area of the attack. Some officials were of the view that it was the handiwork of a nursing tigress which had launched the attack in defence of her cubs.

All this resulted in Dhitoo getting a reprieve. It was supposedly his first human kill, and guidelines specified that a tiger can be condemned as a man-eater only after he has deliberately made two human kills. Moreover, Dhitoo also happened to be an all-round favourite of the officials, was a prime subject of an ongoing documentary film, and was being baited often as a star attraction for special guests who were captivated by the sight of this magnificent tiger.

But known or unknown to the complicit Corbett Park officials, another grim tragedy involving Dhitoo was in the offing.

CHAPTER 15

Dhitoo, and the Second Kill

It was Babu, a Nepali labourer who became Dhitoo's second kill. Babu was employed as a casual labourer working with one of the road-gangs that are contracted annually by the Corbett Park authorities to build or repair the fair-weather road networks within the Park. At the time of the incident, he was working with his group at Khinanauli FRH area.

One afternoon he arrived at Dhikala on his way back from Kalagarh, where he had gone to see his family. These casual daily-wage labourers are not allowed leave of any kind, but they usually make arrangements with their colleagues to work double-time or stand in their place, so that they can make short journeys back to their families, and attend to their immediate needs.

At Dhikala, he made a short stop at Buddhi Kala's canteen for a cup of tea. Ishtiaq and a couple of his friends also were there, and they exchanged greetings with Babu. On being asked how he came to be at Dhikala, Babu informed them that he would be on his way to Khinanauli as soon as he had completed his tea. Greetings over, off he went walking the forest road to his destination.

He reached Khinanauli FRH in the evening, before darkness had fallen, and spent the night in the company of other labourers in the room allotted to them. But tragedy awaited him next morning, when he went down to the Ramganga river flowing below the forest rest house. It seems that as he was bent double while collecting fire-wood near the wooden plank bridge built across the river, he was suddenly attacked by a tiger and quickly carried away.

Dr Rastogi, a guest staying at the Khinanauli FRH, was at that time out on the morning elephant safari and returning from the Taulia Road. Rastogi distinctly heard a single human cry yelling *"bachao"* (save me). He mentioned this to his mahout, but since he had heard nothing, Rastogi also became doubtful about the occurrence.

But he continued to have a nagging thought that since their elephant was wading across the river at the time the scream was heard, it was quite possible that the mahout had then been busy guiding the elephant cross the river, and so missed hearing the scream due to the sound of the gushing water.

When the river had been crossed, and they were passing by the wooden plank bridge where Babu had been taken by the tiger, they came upon a single shoe and from there on, clear drag mark leading from there to a nearby clump of bushes. The sight of the shoe and the drag mark along the road, was now enough confirmation for Rastogi and the mahout that the single shout for help which he had heard, had been for real.

So they followed the drag mark left by the tiger carrying his human kill. The drag mark then left the road and went down the right side into a small *nullah* covered with thick undergrowth. There, lying with the dead man was the tiger, growling at them for intruding. Without wasting any time, they quickly backed away and reached the Khinanauli FRH to sound the alarm.

A wireless message was sent to Dhikala where the Field Director CB Singh was also camping at that time. A message was also sent to Brijendra Singh, who responded that he was starting forthwith for Khinanauli. The Director deputed AN Singh to reach the kill site and ensure that the tiger and his kill was closely monitored till the Director arrived there.

AN Singh arrived at Khinanauli riding Ishtiaq's elephant Rambha, along with a team of five other mahouts on their elephants. As soon as they saw the tiger, they identified him as Dhitoo. He was in his usual fearless and belligerent mood, and refused to relinquish his kill, snarling at the elephants which were trying to drive him away from the human body.

They only succeeded when Dhitoo finally left the kill and went down to the river for a drink. After he had gone, the elephants were made to surround Babu's body to protect it. It had by then been largely eaten by the tiger, and only a small part of one foot and the upper torso remained.

It now seemed a pretty long wait for the mahouts till the other officials arrived there. To while away the time, AN Singh reclined in the *howdah* of the elephant he was mounted on, even as Ishtiaq kept up the vigil. Suddenly, they became aware of a constant jerking of Rambha's body, who was continuously kicking out with her hind legs.

At first, they thought she was being pestered by flies and was trying to get rid of them. But it was only when she suddenly let out a loud trumpet and swerved around, that Ishtiaq saw that it was actually the tiger which was trying to get past the elephant's feet and reach his kill. However, now that the rescue party had become aware of the Dhitoo's efforts to reclaim his kill, they once again drove him away and tightened their circle of defence.

At about 2 pm Brijendra Singh arrived at the place along with the Field Director and other staff members. On surveying the area and analysing the possible course of action, they decided to arrange for a bait and trap-cage so that the belligerent Dhitoo could be trapped at the spot.

Babu's body was removed from there for handing over to his family for the last rites. Two people got down from their elephants and quickly loaded the remains of the victim onto one of the elephants. At such times the mahouts usually carry a large sack which is used to carry the mangled remains of a tiger's victim.

The party of elephants left with the body for Dhikala, while Ishtiaq was ordered to stay back with his elephant at the site to keep a watch on the tiger's movement. As soon as the other elephants moved away from the spot Ishtiaq positioned his elephant a short distance away from where the body had been lying. He then saw Dhitoo immediately rushing to the spot whether he had been earlier feeding on his kill. Not finding it there, he started quartering the place in short circles, and then started moving on the track which the departing elephants had taken.

Since Dhitoo was now moving away and was not likely to remain at that spot any more, Ishtiaq also followed it at a safe distance. After some time, the tiger disappeared into the forests near the Khinanauli FRH, and Ishtiaq made his way back to Dhikala.

CHAPTER 16

Dhitoo's Capture

Now that Dhitoo had deliberately made his second human kill, he could now be categorised as a man eater. Once that decision was taken, it was a foregone conclusion that he would now be captured and removed from Corbett National Park.

The method of his capture involved the procurement of live baits that would be used to lure him in a cage having a trapdoor that would fall into place when he entered the cage to reach the bait. Ishtiaq recalls that when the bait was being put up in the cage Dhitoo was prowling around close by, and seemed absolutely intent on entering the cage and killing the bait right away.

It was a tense moment for the staff members who were down on the ground making the cage ready with the buffalo calf inside, and setting up the trigger that would drop the trapdoor when Dhitoo stepped in to kill the bait. The officials ordered that two vehicles and two elephants be positioned such that they could prevent Dhitoo from making any sudden attack on either the bait or the staff. It was only the presence of the vehicles and elephants that kept him at bay.

Park Director Ashok Singh, Deputy Director RN Pandey, Brijendra Singh and AN Singh were present at the spot. Once the cage was set, the elephants and staff members were ordered to leave the place. While this was being done, Brijendra Singh had stationed his vehicle a little distance away and camouflaged it so that he could stay at the place and record the events of Dhitoo's capture as they happened. It was into this vehicle that all the officials retreated to await the capture. It was expected that Dhitoo would rush into the cage as soon as the elephants and vehicles blocking his way were withdrawn from the place.

When these restraints were finally removed and Dhitoo had a clear field to approach the cage, some instinct made him cautious. He approached the cage twice, but retreated without actually entering it. It was only on the third approach that he finally rushed in to reach at the bait, the trapdoor fell into place, and Dhitoo's angry roars resonated in the forest to announce that he had been finally captured.

Hearing his roars, the staff and elephants returned from the place nearby, where they had stationed themselves to await Dhitoo's self-entrapment. Ishtiaq recalls that when they reached the cage, Dhitoo was in a fit of rage, clawing and biting at the bars, and instinctively trying to insert his paws and nose under the trapdoor in a bid to lift it.

The trapdoor had still not been secured, so Ishtiaq climbed up on top of the cage to tie it so that it could not be lifted. However, seeing him on top, Dhitoo reached up in an effort to rake Ishtiaq through the bars. Sensing his predicament and the imminent danger of him being clawed by Dhitoo, the officials quickly had a vehicle seat thrown on top of the cage, and instructed Ishtiaq to step on it so that he could stay away from the sharp raking claws of the tiger. This provided a secure foothold, and Ishtiaq was then able to secure the trapdoor from being lifted by the angry tiger.

Now came the problem of lifting the cage with its angry roaring inmate, and putting it into a truck for being transported back to camp. This was accomplished only after AN Singh tranquillised Dhitoo to make him sleepy and less aggressive towards the humans who would be handling the cage, and also to prevent the tiger from hurting himself any further with his violent attacks on the cage bars.

Soon after his capture, he was transported by truck to Lucknow, and temporarily kept in the Prince of Wales Zoological Gardens. After a brief stay at Lucknow Zoo, he was finally sent to Kanpur Zoo where he spent his last days.

This brings me to my own encounter with Dhitoo. As soon as I came to know that Dhitoo had arrived at Lucknow Zoo, I went there to see him. He was being kept in one of the regular tiger houses in the zoo, which have small barred rooms for feeding and quarantining of tigers, and a lot of open area in the front for the captive tigers to roam around.

But since Dhitoo was a newly captured wild tiger, and a maneater to boot, he was being kept in solitary confinement within one of the concrete rooms, away from public eye. The bars of his room which faced the visitors' side were shut by rickety wooden panels. Although visitors were not allowed to see him, I reasoned with the keeper and he let me in.

It was dark inside his cell. Leaning against the outer iron railing, and bending double over it to get nearer to the wooden windows, I tried to peer in through one of the cracks in the wood. My eyes could not adjust to the darkened interior at first, so I found it difficult to see him. There was not the slightest sound from inside the cage to let me know whether was tiger was active or sleeping.

But I kept peering in, and as my eyes focused, I saw a single yellow eye smack against the same crack, looking intently back at me. He was doing it so silently that I jerked back hastily in fear, and literally shivered. I came away shaken, without seeing him that day, but did make the keeper promise that he would let me see him again in a couple of days.

He smilingly agreed. Maybe he was laughing at my obvious discomfiture. *"Bohot badmash tiger hai yeh"* (he is a very wicked tiger) he said to me. As if I didn't know, I thought to myself.

Dhitoo in Lucknow Zoo

On the next occasion, when I went to see him about a week later, I saw that he had been transferred to an adjoining iron cage, which had long bars in front that extended over to the roof. There was no place for him to hide from our view. Not liking his stark visibility, he was sitting crouched in a far corner, large and angry. At our approach, he started to emit a deep, low growl.

I was alone with the keeper, and this time he was ready to show me more. He leaned against the outer railing and blew out air noisily from his mouth at him. Immediately Dhitoo was at the bars in a flash, roaring and spitting, stopping to stand full length against the bars. That huge body, the angry visage and the gigantic forepaws were a sight that I'll never forget. It brought out a strong and clear image of the power of a wild tiger, as well as the utter helplessness of its prey, animal or human, when it launches that final attack.

He probably remained as aggressive as he was that day. I say this because he was never displayed as a zoo specimen, but was always kept away from the public gaze. Later he was transferred from Lucknow Zoo to the Kanpur Zoo, about 87 kms away. It was a very large zoo and being newly built, had much better facilities for animals. I specifically went to see him after seeking permission from Mohammed Ahsan IFS, the Zoo Director.

Even there, he was kept away secluded from the public. I was allowed to go in and see him in the area he was housed. Although he was not charging viciously at anyone coming to stand by his cage, he still kept up a continuous low-decibel growl as soon as he saw us. His body had marginally thinned, but the growl and the paws were the same.

It is never a good sight to see a caged wild animal. I never thought of him as being miserable, because a majestic tiger like Dhitoo just can't look that way. Fortunately, soon after, he developed an infection in his tail and died. Thankfully, not too much of his life was spent in captivity and it was good that death brought him release from his unnatural confines. May Dhitoo now always roam free, and hunt in paradise.

Mohammad Ahsan IFS, in his book *The Wild Tales*, mentions that he had first seen Dhitoo in the wild at Corbett Park, and later again when Dhitoo was captured and sent to Kanpur Zoo during his tenure as Zoo Director.

He writes, *"In the month of February 1986 I was transferred from Pilibhit to Kanpur as Director, Kanpur Zoological Park. And here once again I was face to face with this tiger. The staff at Kanpur Zoological Park had many stories to tell of this tiger. It was a very powerful and ferocious animal. In the beginning when it was brought to Kanpur Zoo, it refused to eat anything. It growled so loudly that even the bravest of human beings would shudder.*

This tiger did not like dressed buffalo meat fed to him like other tigers in the Zoo. It was said that because of this reason, the previous Zoo Director offered him a live neelgai calf which it devoured in no time. But later, offering live animals was discontinued because of public outcry.

The stories told by the staff were true. It was really a beautiful animal and indeed very powerful. When it roared loudly, visitors were often seen running away in terror, despite the fact that they knew the tiger was in captivity and could not escape the enclosure. Gradually it adjusted itself to a life of captivity. Dhitoo later mated with a zoo bred tigress Sundari and sired two cubs. A few years later, it died of some ailment, the exact details of which have eroded away from my memory."

And thus ended the saga of the infamous Dhitoo, the stubborn tiger of Corbett Park.

CHAPTER 17

Taimur – in the Footsteps of Dhitoo

Having recounted to us his versions of the exploits and misdemeanours of Dhitoo, Ishtiaq then mentioned the tiger named Taimur, who he said was Dhitoo's cub.

It came as a surprise to me since I never had any knowledge or recollection of the existence of such a tiger. I could also not believe that there was any study or analysis done in those times which could determine the family tree of tigers born in Corbett Park. It was not just Ishtiaq who would be ignorant on that count, but there could no other person who knew the truth of this contention. Which tigresses Dhitoo mated with, and which tigress gave birth to Taimur were all matters of hearsay.

With that issue set aside, I did look forward to an interesting tale of a tiger that the staff of Corbett Park credited as being Dhitoo's cub. Our interest soared at the mention of this tiger, and we urged Ishtiaq to tell us about the son of Dhitoo. Ishtiaq was glad to do so.

Like his father, Taimur was also a robust and well-built male who frequented the *chaurs* or grasslands lying below Dhikala and Khinanauli. He also displayed no fear of men and much like his father was also found walking the forest road. He even went a step farther in his boldness than Dhitoo, by also intruding near the premises of the forest rest houses located in his domain.

Suddenly Ishtiaq had a twinkle in his eyes and a mischievous smile of remembrance lit up his face. It was evident to me that an interesting story was about to be narrated. He chuckled to himself as he recounted one funny run-in with Taimur, that also featured AN Singh.

He said that some friends of AN Singh had come to visit Dhikala. As was usually the case, AN Singh requisitioned the services of Ishtiaq and Rambha to take him and his visiting friends on an elephant safari.

The safari started from Dhikala to the Sambhar Road and from there down the incline to the Ramganga river flowing below. The elephant had barely crossed over to the other side of the river when they spotted Taimur sitting in a clump of bushes, gorging on a chital kill. As soon as they approached near the place where he was lying, Taimur got up growling and charged halfway to the elephant It was a clear warning for them to back away. But the patient and brave elephant Rambha was hardly flustered at the tiger's bravado and remained standing steadfast on her spot.

Seeing that his mock-charge had not had the desired effect on the intruders, Taimur came out again roaring and this time rushed close to the elephant. Reaching near, he lifted a great forepaw with claws fully unsheathed, in readiness to lash out at the elephant's trunk or leg. It seemed a dangerous situation now, so Ishtiaq took evasive action by swerving the elephant broadside on, to get her trunk and front legs out of range of the great swiping paw. However, this sudden swerve of the elephant brought one of the riders - a friend of AN Singh who shall remain unnamed - onto the side of the angry tiger. The scared gentleman instinctively leaned backward on the howdah, lifting both his feet above the footrest. The suddenness of the move resulted in him being unsettled on the howdah, and with no foothold for his feet, he fell back on the howdah with both feet in the air.

This ignominious position was further compounded when he involuntarily let out a loud fart. AN Singh was never one to let go of such a chance of pulling his friend's leg, and as the poor man was discomfited and embarrassed by his ungainly position, and the loud sound that had emanated from him, AN Singh let him have a choicest expletive followed by *"Abey kya kar raha hai? Sher ko apne 'misfire' se dara raha hai?"* (What do you think you are doing? Trying to scare off the tiger with your misfire?). His absolute discomfiture was further compounded by the presence of a lady in the howdah who also joined in the loud guffaws at his expense.

Down in the grass, the tiger must have also felt insulted at this sudden and complete loss of interest that the humans suddenly displayed in him, and he quietly slunk back to his kill, while the resilient Rambha plodded back toward camp with the very red-faced friend. Ishtiaq says that even after they arrived back at camp, AN Singh continued to rib his friend by bringing up the incident of the 'misfire'.

Taimur's area extended to Bichubhoji, and he was very frequently seen there for almost one and a half years. During that period, he made it a habit to lie throughout the day under a shady tree by the roadside. This behaviour became a boon for tourists, who would be brought there by the drivers, guides and mahouts, and then they would have a great time in photographing Taimur.

Then some tourists got so emboldened that they got off their vehicle and started walking towards Taimur to try and get a closer shot. When this was brought to the notice of authorities, they promptly placed a ban on tourist vehicles approaching Taimur since they feared that if this kind of intrusion continued, Taimur might one day get caught up in a situation where he might launch an attack on some offending tourist who came too close. The saga of David Hunt was fresh in everyone's mind and the authorities were fearful of such an incident being repeated once again.

A further development in Taimur's bold ways resulted in him often coming quite close to the Dhikala camp. This put a scare in the families of the staff posted at Dhikala, and they complained to Range Officer Nautiyal. He urged them to submit a written application which could then be taken up with the senior officials. The Park Director Ashok Singh considered the application favourably and ordered that all underbrush around the camp be cleared so that Taimur could not get any camouflage from where he could launch an attack.

I asked Ishtiaq if Taimur's forays near the camp occurred only at night, but was informed that he used to come near the camp even in broad daylight. He would choose a tree near the road to Dhikala and sit there watching all the human activity going on in camp. Ishtiaq himself saw Taimur sitting near the camp many times.

Once he was out on his elephant with an official and saw Taimur sitting in the grassland. There was also a herd of chital grazing nearby, fully aware of the tiger's presence. But the chital were not alarmed since they instinctively knew that the tiger was not on the hunt. The official asked Ishtiaq to drive the chital towards Taimur in the hope that they might see him making a kill. The herd ran by close to the tiger, but he did not make any attempt to hunt them. Ishtiaq commented to the official that 'our Taimur is quite like the nawabs of Lucknow who would take a mouthful of grapes only when the bunch was dangled near their face'.

One day Ishtiaq was out in the company of AN Singh when they saw Taimur sitting in the grass. Their elephant's approach alarmed a herd of chital grazing in the neighbouring grassland

and they bolted at the elephant's approach. One chital fawn ran right towards the place where Taimur was sitting and almost banged into the tiger. Taimur hardly moved. All he had to do was place a large paw on the fawn, pinning it down.

A little later he leisurely picked up the fawn and slumped down some distance away in the grassland. He must have been feeding for about 20-30 minutes when a tusker ambled into the grassland, walking in the general direction where Taimur was feeding. Both Ishtiaq and AN Singh anticipated that this encounter of a tusker and a feeding tiger would at least lead to remonstrations by both but the tusker emerged on the other side of the grassland while Taimur continued to have his lunch peacefully.

Ishtiaq on Rambha, combing the Dhikala chaur.

This does indicate that Taimur was a much more even-tempered tiger as compared to his alleged father Dhitoo. It was expected by all the staff members at Corbett Park that Taimur would play a dominant role for a long time, but that was not to be. Quite suddenly, Taimur ceased to be seen along the pathways and grasslands that he usually frequented. He disappeared from the scene, never to be seen again. Whether he was poached or died a natural death could never be ascertained or recorded.

CHAPTER 18

The Tragedies of Life

It was the day before *Baqreid* (Eid-ul-Adha). Ishtiaq had to go to his home in Ramnagar to celebrate the festival with his family. He took his elephant from Dhikala to Dhangarhi gate and left it there in the care of his *characut* for the couple of days that he would be away. He then went on to Ramnagar and stayed for the next two days with his family.

On the morning of the third day, Ishtiaq had to return to resume his duties at Dhikala. As he prepared to leave his residence at Ramnagar, his youngest son Ahsan, who was seven years old at that time, hung on to him, requesting him to take him along to Dhikala. So Ishtiaq asked his wife Razia to make arrangements for the little boy to accompany him. Razia did so but mentioned that since the boy usually did not go anywhere without his elder sisters, it would be better if they were taken along too. Finally, Ishtiaq, his little son, and two daughters boarded the bus from Ramnagar to Dhangadhi gate, where Ishtiaq's elephant was quartered.

Mounting the elephant, all of them started on the journey to Dhikala. It was a wonderful experience for the kids, who asked their father to stop now and then to either admire the wildlife that came into view or to pick a few wild fruits off the trees that grew along their path. The kids' picnic continued as they had a good time at Dhikala, playing with children of the other staff members there. After a few days, the other two sons of Ishtiaq – Irfan and Rizwan – also came to Dhikala to spend some time with their father, and life went on with fun and games for the kids.

Ishtiaq with his wife Razia and his three sons.
Little Ahsan is in Ishtiaq's lap.

It was around the eleventh day of their stay in Dhikala that a terrible tragedy befell Ishtiaq. That night too, Ishtiaq had trussed up his children in bed and put up a mosquito net to protect them from being bitten by mosquitoes. At about 2.30 AM one of his daughters cried out fearfully to Ishtiaq that Ahsan had been bitten by a snake. Ishtiaq sprang out of bed, putting on the light to see what had happened. He could see the snake that crept out of the children's mosquito net and slithered into a canvas bag kept on a chair beside the bed.

Ishtiaq's immediate reaction was to run to the neighbouring shack of Eidu mahout, to ask if he had some anti-venom. But Eidu had nothing of that sort with him. By this time, word had spread among the mahouts and *characuts* living there, and most of them rushed to Ishtiaq's shack. The snake was located outside the shack and promptly dealt with. But the worrisome discovery that came to light was that the snake happened to be a mid-sized hamadryad (*Ophiophagus hannah*) or king cobra.

Seeing the puncture marks on Ahsan's hand, a tourniquet was quickly tied on his arm by Ishtiaq's *characut* Ganga Ram. He belonged to the little town of Kaladhungi (where Jim Corbett's winter home is situated), and was credited with having a cure for snake-bite. Ganga Ram prepared a potion of neem (*Azadirachta indica*) leaves and forced it down the little lad's throat. It was common folk-lore that if a poisoned person is fed with the neem-leaf potion, he would not find it bitter, but sweetish. Ahsan was constantly trying to spit out the potion, all the while complaining that it was too bitter. He then totally refused to put any more in his mouth. A little while later, the boy's hand started to swell because of the tightness of the tourniquet.

He started crying and asked Ishtiaq to open the tight knot. But Ishtiaq did not want to do that for fear of the venom spreading in the body. Some voices clamoured that the arm should be given an incision to draw out the poisoned blood, but Ahsan heard that and clung to Ishtiaq asking him not to have his hand cut. In this confusion, some dominant voices prevailed upon Ishtiaq to open the tourniquet. When he tried to untie it, the hand had swollen so much that it was impossible to untie the knot. So it was finally cut with a pair of scissors.

Ishtiaq says that hardly three minutes had elapsed since opening the tourniquet that the little boy seemed to lose his sight. This became evident when Ishtiaq handed him a cup with some sweets to eat. Ahsan could not even see the cup in Ishtiaq's hand and started floundering for it. Now in a great state of panic and despair, Ishtiaq ran to the quarters of Tara Dutt Joshi who was posted as a guide in Dhikala, to request him to arrange for the department's motorboat so that he could take his son by boat to Kalagarh. This would be a quicker and shorter way to reach a place where some medical help could be found for the boy.

Quickly, some diesel was arranged for the boat, and an elephant was readied to take the patient to the boat which was moored about one and a half km away on the reservoir near Leedkhalia. Mounted on the elephant, Ishtiaq started for the boat holding his little son to his chest. His two daughters and two sons also accompanied him since they did not want to be left alone at Dhikala. A few concerned staff members also walked along with the elephant to see Ishtiaq off to the boat.

On the way, the little boy threw his hands around Ishtiaq's neck, and bringing his face close, started kissing his father's face. Ishtiaq patted him, all the while assuring his boy that things would be alright soon. Once again Ahsan tried to left himself up and bring his face to Ishtiaq's, but this time he fell backward and lay supine in Ishtiaq's lap. Seeing him in this condition, Ishtiaq's heart was filled with dread, and he could only mutter in a broken voice, "*Ahsan beta, kya tum humein chhor ke aise chaley jaoge?*" (Son, will you leave us and go away like this?). When they reached the boat and the lad was brought down from the elephant onto the boat, he was almost dead.

The boat carrying Ishtiaq and his children started for the Saddle Dam, which was the disembarkation point. From there a bus plied to Kalagarh, but since it was a Sunday, it was not operating that day. However, two staff members who had been informed about Ishtiaq's arrival, came by bicycle from Kalagarh to be at hand. Carrying the limp body of his little son in his hands, Ishtiaq was now walking dazedly towards Kalagarh. He had no idea what to do, and all he did was to request the two staff members to carry his other children on their bicycles to Kalagarh.

At Kalagarh, Ishtiaq reached the house of Shafi mahout and placed his son's body there. As staff members started gathering in Shafi's house, there were again differing opinions. Someone ran and brought over the village doctor, who confirmed the demise of the boy. Someone else brought a local snake charmer, who also confirmed the worst.

The Deputy Ranger posted at Kalagarh at that time was Karmiyal. He had a long association with Ishtiaq's children since they had been posted together for a long period. Karmiyal's wife was unable to come to terms with the tragedy that had struck Ishtiaq, and she started wailing loudly. Ishtiaq was by now thunderstruck by the tragedy, but he told her to desist, otherwise, he too would also lose his composure. How would he then go all the way to his home in Ramnagar and face his wife and children with the body of his dead son?

As he started on his journey to Ramnagar, Karmiyal's wife insisted on giving him five hundred rupees to help Ishtiaq during the journey. Ishtiaq wanted to hire a bus, but when the bus driver saw the body, he insisted on an exorbitant payment of Rs 2000. However, a forest guard named Heera Singh Bisht came to Ishtiaq's aid and offered to take them to Ramnagar on his motorbike. So Ishtiaq sat on the pillion seat and started his journey to Ramnagar with his little son's body in his hands.

As the motorbike reached Jaspur, it developed some snag and they had to call a halt to have it repaired. While the roadside mechanic repaired the motorbike, Ishtiaq lay the body on the ground and waited. Soon the motorbike was repaired, and they were ready to continue their journey. Ishtiaq remembers that the mechanic was so sympathetic to their woes that he did not charge anything for his services, and hurried them on their way.

Eighteen km before Ramnagar, Ishtiaq's hands and feet were aching with the effort of carrying his sons' body in his hands.

So he asked Bisht to make a stop so that he could rest his aching and weary body. Once again, they stopped by the roadside. Once again, the dead body was placed on the roadside while Ishtiaq rested for a while. He was dreading the shock and horror that awaited his wife and children when they came face to face with the grim tragedy that had befallen them. When eventually the motorbike arrived at their house in Ramnagar, he entered with little Ahsan's body in his hands.

What transpired in there must have been so painful that its mere recollection prevented Ishtiaq from continuing with the narration. He literally broke down, holding his face in his hands, as great sobs wracked his body. It was natural that the extreme tragedy of events that we were hearing, had been tugging away at our hearts too. But when Ishtiaq broke down, both Tariq and I could not keep our own emotions in check. Tariq left the scene quickly, ostensibly to fetch a glass of water for Ishtiaq, while I just sat dumbly, holding on to Ishtiaq's shoulder in a bid to console him, as well as to seek some for myself too.

It was after a while that Ishtiaq slightly recovered, but we told him to stop the narrative and take a much-needed break from those terrible memories. An intense bout of coughing had seized him while he was crying, and his body now seemed quite starved for oxygen.

Hours later, we composed ourselves to continue with the tragic events. The distraught mother and the eldest daughter were inconsolable, and in their grief, kept blaming Ishtiaq for what had happened. Not willing to accept his death, they insisted that little Ahsan be sent to neighbouring Moradabad to some shrine credited with having healing powers. So Ishtiaq arranged for a taxi and requested some family members to take him there.

In the meanwhile, his other two sons also arrived, both with facial and head injuries sustained when the bicycle of the staff member carrying them from Saddle Dam to Kalagarh, met with an accident. Seeing them in their condition, it was now Ishtiaq's turn to be shell-shocked. All the grief and tension he had weathered from the previous night now took its toll, and he fell to the ground with shock. It was then that his wife and other people present in the house realized that Ishtiaq too was in a bad state, and they turned their attention to him and made him lie down in bed to recoup.

By late evening, the persons who had taken little Ahsan to Moradabad in search of some miraculous recovery also returned, and Ishtiaq's family could do nothing but resign themselves to the loss of the young boy. The next morning, Ahsan's little body was laid to rest in the local graveyard at Ramnagar.

By and by, most of the family members put the tragedy behind them, but it was Ishtiaq's youngest daughter Nazia – younger to Ahsan by about a year – who continued to be heartbroken at the loss of her brother with whom she was very close. As a result of her continued depression, she fell ill after three months.

Once again, tragedy awaited Ishtiaq. He borrowed Buddhi Kala's vehicle to carry his sick daughter to the Ramnagar hospital. Unfortunately, before they could reach the hospital she died, and the hospital doctor confirmed that she had been brought dead on arrival. And so, two of Ishtiaq's youngest children – aged seven and six - died within just three months.

A couple of years later, Ishtiaq's family suffered another tragedy. His third eldest daughter Rabia was cooking in their makeshift kitchen outside Ishtiaq's shack in Dhikala, when her clothes caught fire. Initially, she tried to douse the flaming garment herself, but then her shrieking calls were heard by the eldest daughter, who quickly wrapped her in a blanket. But in the process, she was burnt on her chest and stomach areas.

Deputy Director RN Pandey, whose residence was located at the western edge of Dhikala, near the staff quarters, heard the commotion and himself came running to investigate what the shouting was all about. When he saw Ishtiaq's daughter with her burn injuries, he immediately requisitioned his vehicle to take the girl to Ramnagar hospital. Once again, Ishtiaq and his wife were on another grim journey to the hospital, with dark forebodings in their hearts. Reaching Ramnagar, the daughter was admitted to the hospital and her treatment was started.

Ishtiaq's friends and relatives gathered in the hospital to visit the child. They assured him that they would all be at hand to look after her. Convinced that she was in good hands, Ishtiaq returned to Dhikala to resume his duties.

After three days he received an urgent message from his wife that their daughter's condition was deteriorating, and that he should come immediately to Ramnagar. Starting soon after receiving the message, Ishtiaq managed to reach the hospital by 9 PM.

Reaching the hospital, he found his family and friends present there. Seeing them all gathered there at that late hour, Ishtiaq had the dark thought that surely his daughter was dead. As the crowd made way for him, he reached his daughter's bed. She saw him and held out her arms towards him, saying in a weak voice, "*Papa mujhe bacha lo*" (Papa, please save me). Ishtiaq hugged her as best as he could and assured her that now that he was with her, he wouldn't let anything happen to her.

But as he came in close contact with his daughter while hugging her, he felt a strong smell of septicaemia emanating from her wounds. In a fit of anger, he accosted the physician attending on her and severely threatened him for his negligence in letting the girl's wounds get so aggravated.

Sensing his disturbed state of mind, the junior doctor present there - Dr Durgapal - intervened and dissipated the tense situation by assuring Ishtiaq to not worry anymore, since he would himself take personal charge of her treatment from now on. True to his promise, Dr Durgapal took great care of the girl and succeeded in curing her burns within a month.

On the day of her discharge from the hospital, a happy Ishtiaq went to Dr Durgapal to thank him for his care and concern, which the good doctor accepted gracefully. Ishtiaq remembers that one month after his daughter's discharge from hospital, Dr Durgapal attained promotion and was transferred to Almora, a posting that he was looking forward to.

When Ishtiaq and his daughter went to bid him adieu, the doctor told them that he was quite convinced that his promotion and transfer was a result of all the heartfelt prayers their family has sent out for him.

 It stands to reason when one hears Ishtiaq speak so highly of Dr Durgapal. Having already lost two children previously, the recovery of his daughter at the hands of the doctor must have come as such a relief for Ishtiaq and his wife.

If Dr Durgapal ever happens to read these lines, he can take a silent bow. His care and concern for a poor man's daughter a long time ago, have earned him cascades of thanks and good wishes.

CHAPTER 19

The Routines of a Mahout's Life

The life of a mahout is not an easy one. He has to manage and control an animal whose size is colossal. A voracious appetite makes the elephant spend most of its waking hours feeding, and its daily needs for rations and green fodder run into gigantic proportions. It also needs its daily bathing and cleansing rituals performed by either the mahout or his *characut*. If it suffers an ailment, the mahout has to nurse it back to fitness with constant care and native remedies.

Mahouts sometimes have to work round the clock in the care and management of their elephants. The 'reward' of all this hard work is the scanty pay they receive, and their low social status in the department. No wonder then that mahouts are now a dying breed. Ishtiaq explained that it was for these reasons that none of his sons showed interest in continuing in their father's profession.

In outlining the inherent pros and cons of a mahout's life, I was fortunate to receive a deep insight provided by Mohammed Ahsan, IFS. As a long-serving officer of the UP Forest Department, he has attained the highest positions during his tenure of service, and with his vast field experience, is well-qualified to talk on the subject of elephants and mahouts. Readers would find his viewpoint full of insight and knowledge, and he has granted me permission to quote him here.

Mohammed Ahsan, IFS says, "*The occupation of mahout in India is as old as the art and science of domesticating wild elephants in the Indian subcontinent. This is as ancient as the*

Indian civilization itself – thousands of years old. The elephant itself has been part of Indian religions, mythology, scriptures, folktales, culture, warfare, and lifestyle. Owning an elephant has always been a matter of pride, a symbol of eminence and social status in Indian society. This has been going on for ages. Elephants are worshipped and venerated by Indian masses.

Elephants have been used in warfare since ancient times. In ancient India, say in the Mauryan period, all the land in the country was vested in the king. And the king always had some special forests for the preservation of elephants. Killing an elephant or setting fire to Elephant Forests was a serious offense, warranting capital punishment. In a nutshell, the king had the monopoly over all elephants in the kingdom. Each king maintained elephant stables, their size depending upon the number of elephants pressed into the service of the king. During wars, the elephant brigade formed a solid flank for launching an offensive. Under heavy attack from this flank, the rank and file of enemy armies often got nervous, ran helter-skelter, and were even crushed under the feet of these warring elephants.

And the central character in and around the life of an elephant among all these activities has been the mahout. A mahout happens to be a unique species among men. He is master of all trades relating to an elephant, yet his services have never been sufficiently recognized by the king or the elephant owners, or society at large. A mahout is just a mahout, poorly remunerated in terms of money, and insufficiently recognized in terms of social status. And this has continued for ages.

A mahout figures in the life of an elephant ever since it is born in captivity or caught from the wild. Mahouts are always part of elephant-catching squads that go into forests to catch wild elephants. They are the ones who catch the elephants with the help of other domesticated elephants, put them into temporary captivity under barricades, feed them, and put them under long rigorous training for human use. The mahout knows the anatomy of elephants intimately, he is also the caretaker and indigenous doctor for them; he is their psychologist, dietician, well-wisher, nurse, schoolmaster, and sometimes even foster parent.

The life of a mahout is always very tough. He is on duty twenty-four hours a day. He is on guard at all times. He is exposed to all kinds of dangers, including being mauled or killed by his own elephant, particularly if it is a male and in musth condition; he lives frugally, is lowly paid, and does not command much social status.

The plight of mahouts in charge of elephants employed by temples or private owners in cities or villages, although equally deplorable, is still slightly better off than those employed by the forest department and posted in remote forest areas. The life of a mahout employed in the duty of an elephant in a temple, city, or village has at least some predictable set pattern.

But the life of a mahout in the duty of forest department is unsettled. He lives away from the civilization or any kind of habitation, he is more exposed to dangers of many kinds, including those of wild animals, snakes, and other pests; he is away from his family, his children are not in a position to receive any education, during rains the forests are cut off from all sides, so is he; even getting his ration from village markets becomes difficult. Ironically even if he is hungry himself, he has to first feed tree fodder at least, if nothing else, to his elephant under all conditions. He has to watch his elephant round the clock.

If the place of posting in the forest is as remote as Dhikala, in Corbett National Park, a mahout's plight is compounded many times over. He has no holidays, not even the national holidays, let alone the usual Sundays or other designated holidays. Here the mahout is not only supposed to know his elephant but the fragile terrain of the forest and landscape too. No wonder then, that the art of mahoutgiri is now a dying profession."

With this perceptive background on the living conditions of mahouts, coming from a former Corbett Park Director and a senior-most IFS officer, I move on to my conversation with Ishtiaq.

All in a Day's Work

I asked him to spell out one typical day in the life of a mahout. He said that the mahout would get up from bed at about 5 AM. After his morning ablutions, he goes straight to his elephant, taking along its morning ration of wheat flour *rotis* which had been prepared the night before. He feeds these *rotis* to the elephant by his own hand. This is the primary morsel that has to be fed to the elephant, else it would refuse to eat the green fodder.

The mahout then returns to his room and partakes of his tea and refreshments. He now orders his *characut* to unfasten the elephant from its fastening chains and bring it out of the *feelkhana*. The *characut* now cleans the elephant's back and sides and applies oil and a little colourful decoration to its forehead. The mahout now joins his *characut* to saddle up the howdah.

After the elephant is saddled, the mahout walks it to the mounting station where four tourists would mount his elephant for the morning safari. The mahout will now traverse the forest for three to five km on different terrains, trying to show the tourists all the wildlife there is to be seen during the ride. The elephant ride ends after about three hours and the elephant is brought back to camp.

After the tourists dismount, the mahout unfastens the cot which serves as a seat on the howdah, and hands over the elephant to the *characut*. The *characut* now takes the elephant into the forest to cut green fodder. This activity usually takes two hours after which the elephant, laden with fodder, returns to camp. After off-loading the stack, and removing the rest of the saddle from its back, the elephant is taken to the river and allowed to play in the water, and get a clean scrub from the *characut*. Thereafter, its hobble chains are put on and it is left to graze in the adjoining grassland.

At about 3 PM, the elephant is recalled from its grazing and saddled up again with the howdah, to take tourists out on the afternoon safari. Returning to camp at the culmination of the afternoon safari, the elephant is now freed from all its trappings and led to the *feelkhana* where it is served its evening rations by the mahout. The *characut* would then provide it enough green fodder to let it eat through the night. It is only now that the mahout and *characut* will be free of the day's work.

Ishtiaq admits that the *characut's* duty is the most back-breaking, but since most of them are young and strong boys, earnestly trying to learn the traits of the mahout's profession, they happily go about performing their assigned duties. I asked whether all mahouts necessarily have to go through the grind of being a *characut* before they become good mahouts, Ishtiaq answered in the affirmative. He explained that it is a 'continuum' – a sort of *silsila* – which the *characut* goes through either with his own mahout-father or under some other mahout from whom he learns the tricks of the trade. He reiterated that taking a shortcut out of the grind of *characut* duties would never allow him to develop into a good mahout. Ishtiaq recalled how he was rigorously trained as a *characut* under mahout Latafat Ali in Ramnagar forest division, and from whom he learned his lessons in becoming a mahout.

I wanted to know how another mahout's elephant would respond to him if he went near it. Would the elephant understand that he is a mahout and someone that could be trusted? Ishtiaq said that both horses and elephants recognize this, and both understand that the person who stands before them is a friend who could be trusted.

Haathi Kheenchna

An oft-repeated phrase that cropped up during Ishtiaq's narratives was '*haathi kheenchna*'. It ostensibly meant 'to saddle up the elephant'. I thought it would be instructive to have him explain the process through which a safari elephant is prepared for riding.

The process starts when the elephant is led out of the *feelkhana* in the morning and brought to an open area. At this time, the elephant's back is usually dotted with mud, dry grass, or leaves which it throws on its back in a bid to keep the flies and other biting insects at bay. The first thing the *characut* does is to make the elephant sit down and then he dusts its back and sides with a dry cloth. When the back is clean, a cotton *gadela* (mattress), weighing about 12 kilograms, is put on the elephant.

This *gadela* forms the base over which the other trappings will be put up next. Another mattress called *gaddi,* made of burlap cloth filled with '*patera*' grass is put up over it next. Both mattresses are now tied firmly to the elephant's back through a thick cotton rope that goes around the chest, with the knot tied on the top.

Ishtiaq and other mahouts making a gadda (mattress)

If the elephant is being taken out to cut fodder, the *characut* would take it to the forest, carrying with him his axe, wooden staff, and a blanket.

The axe is used to lop off the leaves and branches, while the wooden staff serves both as a weapon, as well as to untangle the leaves and branches that get stuck in the tree and do not fall on the ground. The blanket serves as a protection from the cold, and at times can be used to cover up against the attack of forest bees which may have been disturbed. It also serves as a diversionary tool in case wild elephants tend to become menacing or give chase. The blanket is then thrown towards them, and while the attacking elephant pauses to vent its anger on this human-smelling thing, the *characut* and his elephant get that vital window of time to make good their escape.

To continue with the process of *haathi kheenchna*; In case the elephant is being made ready for riding by officers or tourists, the next process involves putting up the *khatola,* which is usually an inverted cot with all four legs pointing upwards. These act as the four hand-holds for the riders. This cot is now firmly secured by ropes through four iron loops. Both sides of the *khatola* are provided with a foot-rest plank that is attached with iron chains and serves as a base for the riders' feet.

One more cotton mattress is now placed on the *khatola* to provide a soft seat for the riders. The primary central rope that was first tied across the larger mattresses is used to sling a rope that goes back across the elephant's rump, under its tail. Another rope goes under the neck, and this is used to secure the *kilawa* – the harness that loops down on both sides of the neck and has foot-holds for the mahout's feet behind the ears.

Ishtiaq laughingly explained that the *kilawa* is both the steering wheel as well as the gears of the elephant. It is the proper use of this *kilawa* that determines the efficiency of the mahout's control over the elephant. If the mahout is adept at keeping the *kilawa* tight, and his thighs are firmly holding the elephant's neck in control, little jabs of the toes alone are enough to make the elephant do the mahout's bidding. Ishtiaq explained that great mahouts are those who never usually utter verbal commands, but communicate silently with the elephant through the use of their legs and toes.

I will mention here that I have also been witness to Ishtiaq's prowess with silent commands to Rambha. Once I had dropped my camera lens cover during an elephant safari. It took me some time to overcome my embarrassment at this clumsiness, while I thought about whether I should let Ishtiaq know. When I did tell him in a whisper, some ground had been covered from the point where the lens cover had fallen. Ishtiaq turned around the elephant without a word and backtracked on the way we had come. Still, no command had been uttered, but Rambha's trunk soon curled backward towards Ishtiaq with the lens cover held daintily in its tip. All I could do in amazement and appreciation was to lightly tap Ishtiaq on his shoulder to convey my thanks.

In another incident, a retired Colonel residing just outside the Corbett Park boundary had one day sent a message to the park authorities that Ishtiaq and Rambha be sent to meet him next morning near the Kanda Road. He would be driving there in his Gypsy, where he would then change over to the elephant to track a tiger that had made a kill the previous day, and was expected to be still lying up over it.

As was my wont, I was also at the Dhikala reception, awaiting the arrival of Ishtiaq and Rambha at the mounting station so I could go with them on the morning safari. But I was told that I could not go with them since they had to go without any tourist, to meet the Colonel on his quest for the tiger.

I could not accept that. I was young and brash back then, and my argument convinced Suresh Pant, the safari allotment official, that I could just be the sole tourist to be riding with Ishtiaq to join the Colonel on his mission. What the good Colonel would have to say to this unwanted rider in the howdah would be brazened out with that careless Indian attitude of "*tab dekha jaye ga*" (We'll see when we come to that).

It was an exhilarating ride. Alone on Rambha with Ishtiaq, was a dream come true. Reaching the appointed place, we now waited for the verbal storm that would ensue when the Colonel came and saw me. But he failed to turn up. Ishtiaq was also not one to be too placatory with authority or pompousness. After the required waiting time had elapsed, he decided to wait no more. But before leaving, he had to somehow communicate to the Colonel that he had arrived and waited for him at the rendezvous point. Silent signals were conveyed by Ishtiaq's toes to Rambha's neck. She broke off two adequately sized branches and placed them in a cross formation by the side of the road where we had waited for the Colonel. If at all he did come later, he would read the signs and know that Ishtiaq had come, waited, and gone.

Since the Colonel had failed to arrive, the elephant was now all mine. I beseeched Ishtiaq to take this opportunity to search for the tiger on our own. But the wise man told me to desist. Firstly, we did not know the actual spot of the kill. Moreover, if the Colonel did come now, and found us tracking the tiger, he could blame us for 'intruding' on 'his' territory. So off we went, away from that quest, but on another that was fully our own.

Returning to Ishtiaq's narrative about the *kilawa;* Ishtiaq said that the method of identifying a good mahout is to check the tightness of his *kilawa*. The adept ones would be using a tight and firm *kilawa* while average mahouts would have loose ones. A loose *kilawa* makes for a comfortable ride for the mahout, whereas a tight *kilawa* keeps the mahout's thighs and feet all tensed up with the grip.

While talking to us, Ishtiaq showed the insteps of both his feet which had very prominent calluses formed from years of elephant driving while sitting on a tight *kilawa*.

The State of 'Musth'

Since Ishtiaq always had female elephants in his charge, the obvious question was why no male elephant ever came to be under his control. He explained that as a policy, only female elephants were purchased by the forest department since the nature of work required elephants to be on full time duty. In the case of male elephants, the '*musth*' period produces such a temperamental state of mind that it is not possible to put them to work for as long as the *musth* period lasts.

Musth is a physical and mental condition that afflicts adult male elephants. Temporal glands located on the sides of their foreheads start to swell and a smelly, sticky discharge, rich in testosterone, starts to ooze out from the glands. During this state, the male elephants show a lot of aggression and become sexually active. Usually, the onset of *musth* starts with a three-week pre-*musth* condition, followed by one month of high-*musth*, and tapers off with a one-month post-*musth* condition.

Talking about the sticky discharge emanating from the temporal glands, Ishtiaq explained that this fluid is called '*mudh*', and has its typical specific uses. In olden times it was common for owners of the best fighter cocks and partridges to be somehow associated with members of mahout families, who could get access to this fluid. These bird owners would prepare bird-food pellets made of flour mixed with *desi ghee* and dry fruits. Before feeding the pellets to their bird, they would take out the bottle containing the *mudh*, dip in a match-head, lace the pellet with this secret potion and feed it to the bird. Fortified with this dose of elephant testosterone, their birds would run through their opponents with great gusto. Needless to say, these birds were always the ones to win all the cockfights or partridge fights that they contested.

Ishtiaq recalled that the father-in-law of his elder sister was one such bird owner, whose cocks and partridges were all famous as champions. When asked how this gentleman came into possession of all the *mudh*, Ishtiaq said that in his early years he was a *saathmaar* in the nawab's elephant stables at Rampur, and therefore could get access to all the *mudh* he would ever require. His name was Buddhi Khan and he had a formidable reputation as the owner of champion fighter birds. He was reverently addressed by everyone as *Ustad* (Master).

The Saathmaars

Now 'saathmaar' was a new word for us, and that needed to be explained too. According to Ishtiaq, saathmaars were sort of elephant 'jousters' or 'picadors' employed by the nawabs and rajahs who owned elephants. They were used in a cruel sport played out by elephants and saathmaars. Armed with long spears, the saathmaars were very agile men, and their job entailed bringing a musth elephant to a state of high rage. This they did by riling it constantly with spear jabs and then nimbly running out of reach of the enraged elephant.

The action was played out in an arena where noblemen and the public watched safely from balconies. The arena had a few small pits into which the saathmaar would quickly hide when the enraged elephant came his way. Immediately, another saathmaar would jab the elephant on the other side, and run for safety. This would go on with the maddened elephant bellowing and trumpeting in anger and pain, while the audience raucously applauded the saathmaars for their agility and bravery.

The Taming of a Killer Elephant

The nawab of Rampur's stables had about 50 elephants, and Ishtiaq's maternal grandfather Hidayat Ali and paternal grandfather Ali Hasan were both employed there as mahouts. Ishtiaq's mother used to often tell the story of how her father Hidayat Ali had been given charge of a very temperamental male elephant, which had killed seven of its previous mahouts. When the family members heard that Hidayat Ali had been appointed as mahout to the killer elephant, they all went into shock and mourning. That evening, not a single lamp was lit in their house, so great was the feeling of anxiety and depression about the now-certain fate of Hidayat Ali.

His wife and other family members implored him to leave the job immediately and save himself from certain death. But it seems that Hidayat Ali was made of sterner stuff. He refused to give up the job, saying that his grit and expertise were both at stake. To compound matters, he was also aware that the particular elephant was the nawab's favourite animal, and there were standing orders that the elephant was not to be beaten or ill-treated by any of his keepers.

On the very first night of his duty with this elephant, Hidayat Ali ordered the *characut* to go home, telling him that he needed time and solitude to acquaint himself with the elephant. The *characut* happily accepted this offer, and went away, leaving Hidayat Ali alone with the elephant. The first thing the elephant did when he saw this new man in his stable was to fling its heavy water bucket towards the man. Hidayat evaded the missile and tried to pacify the elephant by talking softly to it, but that did not work and the elephant continued to be belligerent. The wily Hidayat Ali had come prepared for such an eventuality. He had quietly smuggled in an iron spearhead, even though all tools of elephant control were strictly prohibited by the nawab.

Hidayat lashed the spearhead onto a bamboo pole kept in the stable. He then put the spearhead in the fire and heated it till it was red hot. Taking the spear near the elephant's hind side, he called out to him. As the elephant looked back at him in rage with flailing trunk and uplifted tail, Hidayat scored a perfect bulls-eye by shoving the searing spear right into its rectal orifice.

As an aside, let me admit that this narrative, when being recounted by Ishtiaq, could not have been just a straight one. It was amply laced with all his earthy wit and humour. As we listened, both Tariq and I were doubled up with laughter - the intense human cruelty, and the scorching pain of the killer elephant be damned.

The story goes that Hidayat glowingly recounted that as soon as the spear found its target, "*usmay se dhuan nikal gaya*" (the rectum literally smoked). The searing iron made the elephant emitted a great bellow of pain and it fell forward on its forehead. Hidayat knew that the point he wanted to make to this killer elephant had been well scored. He quickly dismantled the spearhead and hid it out of sight.

As expected, the sentry on duty heard the bellowing of the elephant and assumed that the new mahout was ill-treating it in defiance of the standing orders of the nawab. He quickly sent out a message to the nawab's palace that "*Hidayat Ali ne haathi ko itna mara hai ki haathi dakra riya hai*" (Hidayat Ali has beaten the elephant so much that it is bellowing in pain).

It did not take the nawab long to respond to this disturbing news, and he promptly arrived at the stables in his six-horse carriage. On his arrival, he called out angrily to Hidayat Ali asking him how he dared to beat his favourite elephant. But the canny mahout was ready with his reply, "*Huzoor*, how can I manage to beat him when he is not even letting me come near him".

The nawab came in and looked the elephant over for any sign of injury. Not finding any, he seemed satisfied that his new mahout had not been unkind to the elephant. But obviously, the elephant had been branded with a searing memory for life, so when Hidayat Ali shouted at him the command "*Baith*" (sit), the standing elephant almost fell on the ground, with all four feet splayed out. The alacrity of the elephant's response to the new mahout's command did bring a look of perplexity on the nawab's face, but he did not press the issue.

He went away, possibly happier with his own decision of placing the elephant in Hidayat Ali's charge. As he passed by the sentry who had sent the news of the elephants bellowing, the nawab admonished him for communicating wrong information. But the sentry fearfully told the nawab that he was prompted to so on hearing the elephant's painful trumpeting. By now Hidayat Ali was feeling quite cocksure and offered his own explanation to the nawab that the elephant had bellowed possibly because it saw a bad dream while it slept.

It was evident that Hidayat Ali had now effectively 'branded' his authority on the killer elephant. It started looking at his new mahout with respect and fear. But a fallout of this branding was that the burn injury on the anus now started oozing pus on the dung balls. This could be a serious tell-tale sign of Hidayat's cruel action and had to be hidden at all costs. So, for the next few days, he showed his total devotion to the elephant by staying with it constantly. The actual purpose was to ensure that as soon as the elephant let go of its dung balls, Hidayat would quickly smash them and grind them to dust so that any sign of the pus could not be seen by anyone.

And thus, Hidayat Ali's spear job always remained a secret, while the killer elephant never forgot who the real master of the team was. Hidayat Ali's family was most happy that he had been able to master the elephant and that he would not be the eighth in the sequence of mahouts killed by the rogue.

Another person quite happy was the nawab, who thought that he could now display his favourite elephant since it now seemed to be under the full control of his mahout. He summoned Hidayat Ali and ordered him to get the elephant ready for a proposed fight with another one belonging to a neighbouring rajah.

The elephant fight was slated for one and a half months later. The rations for the elephant's preparation included one canister of opium, half a canister of *desi ghee,* and sacks of dry fruits and condiments. Ishtiaq recalls his mother saying that in that period they also consumed good amounts of the goodies which Hidayat Ali used to bring home.

On the day of the elephant fight, the nawab's elephant was the clear winner after engaging in battle for two hours and eventually knocking down the visiting elephant. At the end of the contest, the nawab threw down to Hidayat Ali a pouch containing 501 silver coins as a reward for his fine effort. In addition, he also ordered that for the next two months both elephant and mahout would be sanctioned a double diet as a reward for their valiant efforts.

Ishtiaq ended this story with his usual chuckle, "*Bas wo garam ballam kaam aagaya*" (It was just that hot spear which did the trick), he said.

The Gajmukta

A common myth regarding elephants is the one about *Gajmukta* or 'elephant pearl' which is supposed to be produced in the elephant's head and is credited with having myriad magical and medicinal powers. When I asked Ishtiaq about it, he had no answer since he was not even aware of the existence of such a thing, or the myth related to it.

This brings to mind my own experience when I saw the *Gajmukta*. I was once in Delhi at the office of the Wildlife Protection Society of India (WPSI), in a meeting with late Ashok Kumar, the legendary wildlife-crime crusader, when he got a call from Pradeep Srivastava, DCP Crime Branch Delhi Police, saying that his team had picked up two boys who were posing as sellers of a *Gajmukta*. The DCP wanted Ashok Kumar to come over to his office and check the object that the boys were trying to sell for a phenomenal amount.

I also accompanied Ashok Kumar to the DCP's office. The object that was displayed on his table was egg-shaped, larger than a hen's egg, and had a patchy green and ivory colour. It felt heavy like a bony mass and had a strong smell of cheap perfume.

Ashok Kumar used his Swiss knife to scrape off little slivers from the object, and burnt them in an ashtray. But the smell that came from it was neither that of burnt bone nor burnt hair. The unanimous decision reached at that time was that it was not an actual elephant derivative, and definitely not a Gajmukta. The final verdict however, was to be reached when the DCP sent it for a lab test later. I regret that I did not follow it up and hence am not privy to that information.

The Rescue of a Wild Elephant Calf

One day, Ishtiaq was out on safari duty with a visiting High Commissioner, along with two Indian ladies. At about 5 PM, while they were passing the Phulai Sot area, they suddenly heard the growling of a tiger from the forest on the adjoining ridge. Ishtiaq carefully took the elephant towards the source of the tiger's sound. On reaching the spot, they spotted a small herd of elephants that were grazing in a bunch. But one female elephant was standing apart from them near a large tree. Ishtiaq's immediate surmise was that this female was about to give birth to a calf and was heading to the spot where she would deliver it.

He turned around to the ladies riding with him, and asked if they wanted to see a new-born elephant? They got excited at the prospect and urged him to take them there. The tiger was now forgotten and Ishtiaq's elephant was directed towards the spot where the female elephant was standing.

As they reached the spot, they saw that on one side of the road lay the tiger looking intently at the female elephant as she stood on the other side of the road. Near her, caught up between two stout branches of another tree was a baby elephant. He seemed so securely stuck in the trap that he could not free himself. The scene being enacted was now clear. The tiger had seen the entangled calf and wanted to attack him, but the mother's presence had stalemated him.

When the tiger saw Ishtiaq's elephant approaching where he lay, he quickly got up and made his way into the forest. The riders on the elephant once again turned their focus on the tiger, clicking photographs of the running animal. Ishtiaq then moved towards the mother elephant, shooing her off, and she reluctantly went and joined the herd.

Going near the entrapped calf, he dismounted to take a closer look. It did not take long for him to assess that the calf had very little chances of dislodging himself. Seeing the man so close, the calf let out a loud bleating sound. That was enough to make the mother elephant come running to her baby's rescue. Ishtiaq quickly remounted his elephant and beat a hasty retreat from the area. Back at Dhikala camp, Ishtiaq informed the officials about the trapped calf.

The next morning, they went to the spot and saw the calf still in the same position. This time they were there with seven elephants and adequate staff to launch a rescue operation. While five elephants set up a protective barrier between the elephant herd and the calf, two elephants were used to physically lift the calf by ropes thrown across the upper branches of the tree and take him out of the fork. After releasing him, they put a rope around his neck, tied him to a lead elephant, and walked him back to camp.

All this while, the other riding elephants kept up the barrier against the wild elephant herd, including the mother. She now seemed resigned to the calf's fate. Or maybe her instinct told her that her calf being taken away alive by humans was a far better fate than if it were eaten by a tiger.

Back at Dhikala, the calf was examined thoroughly and it was found to have multiple bruises on his sides as a result of his constant jostling against the forked branches of the tree he was trapped in. The Park Director believed that if this calf was returned to his mother in the existing condition, his wounds would turn septic and he might not survive.

It was decided to nurse him back to health, and Ishtiaq was entrusted with the responsibility of doing so. The calf was named Phool Charan and he was later entrusted to the care of Eidu mahout's son. He was then transferred to Kanpur Zoo, and from there he was finally sent to Dudhwa national park to work as a safari elephant.

CHAPTER 20

The Last Years

Ishtiaq lost Rambha, his favourite elephant and long-standing companion, in 1998. After her death, he did not want to undertake the cumbersome task of taking charge of a new elephant and again go through the tribulations of being her mahout.

He was now advancing in years and his health had been failing since the loss of his elephant. The sudden snapping of the life-bond between man and animal adversely affects both. Ishtiaq confirmed that the exit of Rambha from his life had a traumatic effect on his psyche and he started feeling a gradual ebb in his zest for life as a mahout. Park officials commiserated with his state of body and mind and allotted him light duties as a guide either at the reception or on vehicles that took tourists on jungle safaris.

He continued to live in his shack at Dhikala with his wife. His eldest son Irfan was also posted at Dhikala as a characut and lived there with his wife and children. These small grandchildren became Ishtiaq's constant companions and became his focus of attention, whom he looked after with love and care.

He was slated to retire in 2004 according to his service records, but before that happened, he fell ill with tuberculosis of the bone, and gradually started losing the use of his limbs. This confined his movements further and he had to walk with the support of a walking stick. It was during this juncture in his life that Tariq and I had intervened and called him over to Lucknow for treatment.

A simple ceremony at Dhikala marks the retirement of Ishtiaq.

In accordance with his official birth records, Ishtiaq retired from service in 2004 on reaching the age of superannuation. He was given a simple send off with garlands and speeches at a ceremony arranged by the Park Warden, which also included Suresh Pant and other staff members.

Ishtiaq died in December 2012. The man who had seen Corbett Park as Hailey national park first as a young boy, then as Ramnagar national park as a sprightly young man, and finally as Corbett Tiger Reserve, had returned into the dust of Ramnagar, where he is now buried.

However, not all of Ishtiaq's being is lost. He gave me great memories that I could draw from when I started writing about him. He also left behind his live images and narratives in my video recordings. His voice can always come back to me as he laughed and cried on recollecting his happiest memories and the testing trials and tribulations of his life.

As I end this narrative of the life and times of Ishtiaq, I can only say a silent prayer for him.

"Fare thee well, my friend. May you find eternal peace and salvation in God's Heaven".

CHAPTER 21

An Epilogue

I shall always regret the fact that I could not meet Ishtiaq during his last years. The fault is singularly mine. From being an avid Corbett Park-goer, I gradually weaned myself away from that once heaven-on-earth. I can give an important-sounding reason by ascribing it to my official preoccupations. But the real cause lay in the anathema born out of the drastic changes that had started sweeping across the Park. These changes were a result of the continually increasing footfall of tourism, and the necessary restrictions that the Park management had to impose to keep it under a semblance of order.

Walking out of camp was banned, electrified fences were strung up around the premises effectively blocking the chital and wild boar that usually loitered all around the rooms in Dhikala during the night. Sometimes, they sent out alarm calls just outside the bedroom windows, warning all and sundry that a tiger or panther had come too close in their wake.

The steps from the old FRH compound going down to the river were now gated, with an ominously humorous sign that said, *"Swimming in the river is prohibited. Survivors will be prosecuted."* Imagine how ludicrous it seemed to someone who never thought twice before taking a towel and swimming trunks and breezing down those very steps to stay in the Ramganga river for the entire day. The river had always been our favourite haunt in the old days where we could remain in the gushing waters for the entire day, coming out only when it was time to go for the afternoon elephant safari.

Good Old Days: Standing in front of the Canteen are (L-R) Babulal, Gopal, Budhi Kala, Eidu mahout, Rajiv Kala, Mahavir, Ishtiaq, Sachin and Dan Singh.

Budhi Kala's Canteen now lies desolate. After his death the family moved to Kalagarh.

Returning from the morning safari, there was a simple but sumptuous breakfast waiting at Buddhi Kala's canteen. Our appetites satiated, we had the option of going to the watchtower overlooking the Sambhar Road and spending the day there. All one needed was a good pair of binoculars and the patience to peer through them at the vast expanse of grassland that lay below. Scattered herds of chital, wild boar, and hog deer were always found grazing in the grassland.

From their actions, one could easily know if a predator was around or not. Very often, a tiger could be sighted if he chose to walk across the grassland and ford the river. He would be

lustily heralded by the alarm calls of the herbivores and birds, and that audio-visual treat would be ample reward for the patient watcher on the tower. If elephant herds chose to make an appearance for a river bath, they would be great subjects to observe how each individual behaved differently from the other.

What's more, we could even walk farther along the Sambhar Road, and take that little slope created by the daily passage of safari elephants, and onto the banks of the Ramganga gushing below. Was there fear in our hearts going out on a limb so far afoot? Yes, there was, but we were always buttressed by the numbers that undertook these adventures.

I remember such a trip to those waters in the summer of 1986. My companion and I were just two in number and both had misgivings about our bravado in trudging through the dense forests. But youth quickly dispelled any lurking dangers in our minds. As we walked past under the watchtower, we were hailed by a group of Norwegians up on the tower. While we waited for them, they quickly climbed down and joined us.

They wanted to know where we were walking to. When I mentioned that we were headed down to the river below, they asked if they could join us. Of course, we said. The numbers were about to be buttressed, and our inherent fear of just being two on that walk dissipated.

We all gambolled in the river for a couple of hours, talking and laughing, when suddenly the name of David Hunt cropped up. I unthinkingly told them where David had met with that accident with the tiger. A hush came over the Norwegians. They had heard of that incident. And now they suddenly realized they were themselves somewhere thick in tiger country. A few sentences were exchanged between them in their language, and in a moment, they were out of the water, ready to walk back to camp. Now feeling lonely and unsafe ourselves, my friend and I also dried ourselves quickly and joined the group as we walked back to camp.

As the time for the afternoon elephant safari approached, we would silently descend from the watchtower and walk back to Dhikala camp. My preferred defence on that walk through the tall grass would be to talk audibly so that any predator resting in the grassland would have ample notice that humans were approaching and it could have a chance to quietly slink away.

The afternoon safari would promise another three hours of thrill, always satiating the soul by the time our elephant trudged back to camp. A quick supper later, all the guests in camp would walk to the small thatch-roofed platform which served as an auditorium. A little 8 mm film projector would be then set up by the staff, and we would be regaled by the great wildlife films of those times. *Land of the Tiger* by Belinda Wright and Stanley Breeden for National Geographic, *Tiger Tiger* and *The Leopard That Changed its Spots* by Survival

Anglia Television used to be such apt presentations in that forest setting. I once heard a wild tiger responding from the dark grassland below to the roar of the tiger in the film *Land of the Tiger* being screened.

The film show over, the die-hard wildlifer would then pull up a chair from the auditorium and take his place on the adjacent wooden platform that served as a deck jutting out over the dark forest below. Chital and sambhar calls would inform the silent listener of the grim game of life and death being played out in the dark grassland. An occasional trumpet would announce that either the matriarch of the elephant herd was admonishing her errant young bulls to behave, or just warning the big cat to stay away from her herd. The imagination would be fuelled by various possibilities, and the night would pass in enjoying the mystery of it all.

With changing times, there came the deluge of wildlife films on television and hand-held devices, and the quaintness of that whirring 8 mm projector was lost to the new breed of wildlifers. The old projector was stowed away since it was of no use now. Digital cameras did away with the patience and necessity of framing and composing an artful picture. "Blaze away" was the mantra for the *nouveau* photographer, who was armed with state-of-the-art cameras and lenses that produced innumerable frames to choose from. Zoom lenses could now capture the exact number of moustache hairs that each tiger possessed.

The elusive and mysterious tiger was now laid threadbare and de-mystified by these pioneers of digital tiger photography. All they needed were action shots. A little twitch of the lolling tiger's ear would trigger the sound of whirring motors, giving the proud possessor of the 'picture-machine' hundreds of frames per minute. Back at home, computer software would be used for adding all the untruths that the final outcome could be embellished with. Tiger photographs and movie clips on social media became so monotonous that one now tended to avoid the overkill.

Gradually the number of elephant safaris offered at Dhikala were first reduced, and then totally withdrawn. The thrill of that undulating and jaunty elephant ride traversing the impenetrable forest tracks was lost to those of us who revelled in the old-world mystique of it all.

Elephant safaris used to make us feel one with the forest. The forest seemed to grow all around as we ducked our heads to avoid being brushed by the looming branches. Wildlife would come within good visual range, being quite unconcerned by the approach of the elephant. The grasslands could be tramped through and the thick lantana bushes could be beaten to reveal the animals hiding there.

But all of that changed. Convoys of Gypsies were now scampering on forest roads determined to show their eager clients the tiger by hook or by crook. Once sighted, the tiger would be hounded by the Gypsies with their load of chattering tourists and excited shutterbugs.

Because they were so frequently hounded and sighted now, the Corbett tigers started displaying a gradual change of behaviour too. From being secretive and elusive, they were now as starkly visible as were the 'circus' tigers of Bandhavgarh, Ranthambore, and Pench National Parks. I once saw a movie clip of a Corbett Park tigress named "Sharmeeli" (the shy one). She walked for a long time alongside a convoy of vehicles loaded with noisy tourists, calmly stopping now and then to spray on trees and bushes. She seemed unconcerned by all the attention she was getting, and there was nothing shy about her behaviour. But Sharmeeli was what they had named her. Sharmeeli my foot, I thought to myself.

The *tamasha* continues. The fad of wildlife tourism is here to stay, and evolving grotesquely all the while. Generations of tigers have been born and bred by their mothers virtually under the wheels of tourist Gypsies. They know the routine perfectly so there is no need for them to be shy or elusive. The noisy circus of tiger-sighting goes on in every national park twice a day right through the tourist season. Like the cheetah mother in the African savannah depositing her cubs under a safari vehicle for shade and safe-keeping, tigers in Ranthambore are now using the cover of a tourist vehicle to stalk in close to a feeding sambhar before launching the final ambush.

Dejected by it all, the old-time wildlifer has become taciturn and withdrawn himself quietly from the mainstream. For him, there is still pleasure to be had in some remote farmhouse bordering the forest, where he can hear the occasional alarm call of the chital or peafowl and let his imagination conjure up images of the lithe form of a tiger or panther somewhere deep in the forest stalking his prey. Not for him the stark visibility of the tiger in a national park. He is happy with only an indistinct pugmark here and a faint scratch-mark there. That is enough to gladden his heart. It assures him that there are still some natural tigers which remain out there, and continue to leave their dwindling imprints on the shifting sands of time.

~ End ~